Once We Lived

Once We Lived

Ken Stewart

Xlibris Corporation
1-888-795-4274
www.Xlibris.com
Orders@Xlibris.com
74455

Preface

This book is dedicated to my son Jason Stewart, who like his Great, Great Uncle Will was taken much, much too early, and to my Great Aunt Violet.

When I think of her, I can still remember visiting her at the age of five to get some of her succulent cookies. I don't remember Aunt Violet only for her cookies but for being the sister of two very brave men, my great uncle Will and Bob.

This manuscript has not been written to make any profit. It was primarily inspired by the thought of providing the relatives of the Fyfe's family with an opportunity to enter some of the memorable moments in the life of William Clifford and Robert James Fyfe who contributed to Canadian history and gave a meaning to Lest we Forget!

John and Annie Fyfe, had a farm on the F & G Side Road, in Richards Landing Ontario. They lived there with their oldest daughter Angus Mary who, I discovered years later, was my grandmother. Angus Mary was followed by five brothers and sisters: William, Robert, Walter, Grace, Violet and George.

Chapter 1—To the Front

- **Private Robert James Fyfe**, born in Richards Landing Ontario, July 1, 1888. Enlisted in the army January 1, 1916 in Sault Ste. Marie Ontario, with the 119th Infantry Battalion: Algoma Overseas Battalion. He reached England in August of 1916, and posted in France as replacement to the 1st Division, 13th Infantry Battalion, Royal Highlanders of Canada by September of 1916.

Figure 1 Regimental Badge Algoma Overseas

As the war progressed and casualties began to mount it became necessary to replace losses in the field with fresh troops. New Battalions like the 119th and the 128th from the 5th Division were now being trained and sent to England as fast as possible. Upon arrival in England most of these new Battalions were absorbed into reserve Battalions. either as reinforcements for the 1st and 2nd Divisions or to the 3rd and 4th Divisions as they were being formed in England.

The original Royal Highlanders of Canada gave birth to three Black Watch Battalions during the war. By the end of August (1914), the regiment numbered over 1,000 men. As the numbers grew, volunteers from the Royal Highlanders were incorporated into the 13th Battalion. Over 60% of the initial recruits were of British origin. A large percentage were former British soldiers who had relocated to Canada at the turn of the century. While still in Canada, the 13th Battalion was placed in the 3rd Brigade of the 1st Division along with the 14th, 15th, and 16th battalions.

The battalion served in France and Flanders with the 3rd Infantry Brigade, 1st Division form February 17, 1915 until the armistice (Royal Highland Regiment—the Black Watch Tartan). Many know the story of the battalion's mascot, a white goat "Flora Stewart" presented to the 3rd by a battalion of Ghurka's. Flora was a war casualty, after eating cabbage poisoned during a gas attack.

- **Private William Clifford Fyfe**, born in Richards Landing Ontario, June 16th 1886. Enlisted in the army April 1, 1916, in Moose Jaw Saskatchewan with the 128th Infantry Battalion. He was transferred overseas and reached France as replacements to the 4th Division, 46th Infantry Battalion on August 11, 1916.

Figure 2 Regimental Badge Moose Jaw

The 46th Canadian Infantry Battalion (South Saskatchewan) was established on 1 February 1915, with its headquarters in the Moose Jaw Armoury. Command was given to LCol Herbert Snell, a Moose Jaw merchant and alderman who, up until then, had commanded the 60th Rifles. The 46th moved to Camp Sewell, Manitoba (also known as Camp Hughes) on 28 May 1915. On 18 October they left for Halifax, sailed for England on 23 October, and arrived at Plymouth a week later. Their strength on leaving Canada was 36 officers and 1115 other ranks. While training in England, parts of the battalion were broken off and farmed out to other units. In return, the 46th received personnel from other battalions such as the 65th Battalion (Saskatoon). They departed from Southampton on 10 August 1916, arriving at Havre in France the next day.

The 46th Battalion served with the 10th Infantry Brigade, 4th Canadian Division from 11 August 1916 until the Armistice. The unit has come to be known as **"The Suicide Battalion"**. The 46th Battalion lost 1,433 killed and 3,484 wounded—a casualty rate of 91.5 percent—and won 16 *battle honours* in 27 months.

The 46th Battalion arrived in France on 11 August 1916, and proceeded directly to the Ypres sector. After five days of "training"— each company taking a turn in the fire trenches, losing in total one man killed and nine wounded in the process—they took their place in the line. After 30 more days at Ypres, and 14 more casualties, the 46th moved to the vicinity of St. Omer. There they exchanged their Ross rifles for Short Magazine Lee Enfields before leaving for the Somme.

ATTESTATION PAPER.

No. 782337
Folio.
Triplicate

CANADIAN OVER-SEAS EXPEDITIONARY FORCE.

QUESTIONS TO BE PUT BEFORE ATTESTATION.
(ANSWERS.)

1.	What is your surname?	Fyfe
1a.	What are your Christian names?	William Clifford
1b.	What is your present address?	Archive Sask
2.	In what Town, Township or Parish, and in what Country were you born?	Richard Landing Ont
3.	What is the name of your next-of-kin?	John Fyfe
4.	What is the address of your next-of-kin?	Richard Landing Ont
4a.	What is the relationship of your next-of-kin?	Father
5.	What is the date of your birth?	June 16th 1886
6.	What is your Trade or Calling?	Farmer
7.	Are you married?	No
8.	Are you willing to be vaccinated or re-vaccinated and inoculated?	Yes
9.	Do you now belong to the Active Militia?	No
10.	Have you ever served in any Military Force? If so, state particulars of former Service.	No
11.	Do you understand the nature and terms of your engagement?	Yes
12.	Are you willing to be attested to serve in the CANADIAN OVER-SEAS EXPEDITIONARY FORCE?	Yes

DECLARATION TO BE MADE BY MAN ON ATTESTATION.

I, William Clifford Fyfe, do solemnly declare that the above are answers made by me to the above questions and that they are true, and that I am willing to fulfil the engagements by me now made, and I hereby engage and agree to serve in the Canadian Over-Seas Expeditionary Force, and to be attached to any arm of the service therein, for the term of one year, or during the war now existing between Great Britain and Germany should that war last longer than one year, and for six months after the termination of that war provided His Majesty should so long require my services, or until legally discharged.

Date April 1st 191 6 .... (Signature of Recruit)
.... (Signature of Witness)

OATH TO BE TAKEN BY MAN ON ATTESTATION.

I, William Clifford Fyfe, do make Oath, that I will be faithful and bear true Allegiance to His Majesty King George the Fifth, His Heirs and Successors, and that I will as in duty bound honestly and faithfully defend His Majesty, His Heirs and Successors, in Person, Crown and Dignity, against all enemies, and will observe and obey all orders of His Majesty, His Heirs and Successors, and of all the Generals and Officers set over me. So help me God.

.... (Signature of Recruit)
Date April 1st 191 6. .... (Signature of Witness)

CERTIFICATE OF MAGISTRATE.

The Recruit above-named was cautioned by me that if he made any false answer to any of the above questions he would be liable to be punished as provided in the Army Act.
The above questions were then read to the Recruit in my presence.
I have taken care that he understands each question, and that his answer to each question has been duly entered as replied to, and the said Recruit has made and signed the declaration and taken the oath before me, at Moose Jaw this First day of April 191 6.

.... (Signature of Justice)
Justice of Peace

M. F. W. 39.
400M.—1 -15.
H. Q. 1772-39-563.

128th (OVERSEAS) BATTLN, C.E.F.
ORDERLY ROOM
APR 4 - 1916
No.
MOOSE JAW SASK.

Figure 3 Side 1 of Williams enlistment documents

Description of William Clifford Fyfe on Enlistment.

Apparent Age. 29 years 9 months.
(To be determined according to the instructions given in the Regulations for Army Medical Services.)

Distinctive marks, and marks indicating congenital peculiarities or previous disease.
(Should the Medical Officer be of opinion that the recruit has served before, he will, unless the man acknowledges to any previous service, attach a slip to that effect, for the information of the Approving Officer.)

Height .... 5 ft. 5½ ins.

Chest measurement:
Girth when fully expanded .... 37 ins.
Range of expansion .... 3 ins.

Complexion .... Light
Eyes .... Blue
Hair .... Light

Religious denomination:
Church of England ....
Presbyterian ....
Methodist .... Yes
Baptist or Congregationalist ....
Roman Catholic ....
Jewish ....
Other denominations .... (Denomination to be stated.)

CERTIFICATE OF MEDICAL EXAMINATION.

I have examined the above-named Recruit and find that he does not present any of the causes of rejection specified in the Regulations for Army Medical Services.

He can see at the required distance with either eye; his heart and lungs are healthy; he has the free use of his joints and limbs, and he declares that he is not subject to fits of any description.

I consider him*. Fit .. for the Canadian Over-Seas Expeditionary Force.

Date .... April 1st .... 1916.

Place. .... Moose Jaw Sask

(signature)
Medical Officer.

*Insert here "fit" or "unfit."

NOTE.—Should the Medical Officer consider the Recruit unfit, he will fill in the foregoing Certificate only in the case of those who have been altered, and will briefly state below the cause of unfitness :—

CERTIFICATE OF OFFICER COMMANDING UNIT.

.... William Clifford Fyfe .... having been finally approved and inspected by me this day, and his Name, Age, Date of Attestation, and every prescribed particular having been recorded, I certify that I am satisfied with the correctness of this Attestation.

(signature)
..........(Signature of Officer)
Lt. Col.,
Commanding 128th.
overseas Batin. C.E.F.

Date .... April 1st 1916

Figure 4 Side 2 of Williams enlistment documents

119TH OVERSEAS BATTALION
ATTESTATION-PAPER.
ORIGINAL

No. 754297

Folio.

CANADIAN OVER-SEAS EXPEDITIONARY FORCE.

QUESTIONS TO BE PUT BEFORE ATTESTATION.
(ANSWER.)

1. What is your surname?	Fyfe
1a. What are your Christian names?	Robert James
1b. What is your present address?	Richards Landing Ont.
2. In what Town, Township or Parish, and in what Country were you born?	Township of St Joe
3. What is the name of your next-of-kin?	John Fyfe
4. What is the address of your next-of-kin?	Richards Landing on
4a. What is the relationship of your next-of-kin?	Father
5. What is the date of your birth?	July 1st 1888
6. What is your Trade or Calling?	Farmer
7. Are you married?	no
8. Are you willing to be vaccinated or re-vaccinated and inoculated?	yes
9. Do you now belong to the Active Militia?	no
10. Have you ever served in any Military Force? If so, state particulars of former Service	2 years in 97. Regt
11. Do you understand the nature and terms of your engagement?	yes
12. Are you willing to be attested to serve in the CANADIAN OVER-SEAS EXPEDITIONARY FORCE?	yes

DECLARATION TO BE MADE BY MAN ON ATTESTATION.

I, Robert James Fyfe, do solemnly declare that the above are answers made by me to the above questions and that they are true, and that I am willing to fulfil the engagements by me now made, and I hereby engage and agree to serve in the Canadian Over-Seas Expeditionary Force, and to be attached to any arm of the service therein, for the term of one year, or during the war now existing between Great Britain and Germany should that war last longer than one year, and for six months after the termination of that war provided His Majesty should so long require my services, or until legally discharged.

Date January 3rd 1916

Robt. James Fyfe (Signature of Recruit)

Sgt. P. Travers (Signature of Witness)

OATH TO BE TAKEN BY MAN ON ATTESTATION.

I, Robert James Fyfe, do make Oath, that I will be faithful and bear true Allegiance to His Majesty King George the Fifth, His Heirs and Successors, and that I will as in duty bound honestly and faithfully defend His Majesty, His Heirs and Successors, in Person, Crown and Dignity, against all enemies, and will observe and obey all orders of His Majesty, His Heirs and Successors, and of all the Generals and Officers set over me. So help me God.

Robt. James Fyfe (Signature of Recruit)

Sgt. P. Travers (Signature of Witness)

Date January 3rd 1916

CERTIFICATE OF MAGISTRATE.

The Recruit above-named was cautioned by me that if he made any false answer to any of the above questions he would be liable to be punished as provided in the Army Act.

The above questions were then read to the Recruit in my presence.

I have taken care that he understands each question, and that his answer to each question has been duly entered as replied to, and the said Recruit has made and signed the declaration and taken the oath before me, at Richards Landing this Third day of January 1916.

W. H. Adams (Signature of Justice)
a Commissioner +

M. F. W. 22.
200 M.—11-15.
H. Q. 1772-10-841.

Figure 5 Side 1 of Bob's enlistment documents

Description of *Robert James Fyfe* on Enlistment.

Apparent Age 27 years 4 months.
(To be determined according to the instructions given in the Regulations for Army Medical Services.)

Height 5 ft. 8 ins.

Girth when fully expanded 38 ins.

Range of expansion 5 ins.

Complexion *swarthy*

Eyes *grey*

Hair *light*

Religious denominations.

Church of England ....

Presbyterian ....

Methodist X

Baptist or Congregationalist ....

Roman Catholic ....

Jewish ....

Other denominations ....
(Denomination to be stated.)

Distinctive marks, and marks indicating congenital peculiarities or previous disease.

(Should the Medical Officer be of opinion that the recruit has served before, he will, unless the case acknowledged to any previous service, attach a slip to that effect, for the information of the Approving Officer.)

Nil.

CERTIFICATE OF MEDICAL EXAMINATION.

I have examined the above-named Recruit and find that he does not present any of the causes of rejection specified in the Regulations for Army Medical Services.

He can see at the required distance with either eye; his heart and lungs are healthy; he has the free use of his joints and limbs, and he declares that he is not subject to fits of any description.

I consider him* *fit* for the Canadian Over-Seas Expeditionary Force.

Date *January 3rd* 1916.

Place *Richards Landing*

James McLean Capt.

B. A. Blackwell
Medical Officer.

*Insert here "fit" or "unfit."

NOTE.—Should the Medical Officer consider the Recruit unfit, he will fill in the foregoing Certificate only in the case of those who have been attested, and will briefly state below the cause of unfitness:—

CERTIFICATE OF OFFICER COMMANDING UNIT.

Robert James Fyfe having been finally approved and inspected by me this day, and his Name, Age, Date of Attestation, and every prescribed particular having been recorded, I certify that I am satisfied with the correctness of this Attestation.

W. W. Rowland Lt.-Colonel,
(Signature of Officer)

O. C. 119th O. S. Battalion, C. E. F.

Date *January 5* 1916.

Figure 6 Side 2 of Bob's enlistment documents

A Brief Outline of the First World War

Defining World War I

Those who fought in WWI believed they were fighting for noble reasons: for defense against aggression, for the love of one's country and for glory. Coming into the war they were fuelled by the ideals of nationalism, liberalism, democracy and religious freedom.

After the Armistice of November 11th 1918, WWI came to be defined by our need to find the meaning for such losses. Exactly what was the significance of the First World War?

Was this not the same message John McCrae had given expression to, three and a half years before Armistice in his poem IN FLANDERS FIELDS?

John McCrae struggled to make some sense out of a senseless war. His plea *"If ye break faith with us who die . . . we shall not sleep"* was made on behalf of the fallen soldiers but it is one that has been embraced by the generations that followed. In this 90th year since the end of WWI (and since the death of John McCrae) the struggle to find some justification for the loss of so many still remains . . . not just in the "War to End All Wars" but in every major conflict since WWI.

WWI—An Accidental War

World War I shaped the 20th century. It launched the United States as a world super power and helped commonwealth countries like Canada, Australia and New Zealand find a sense of National Identity. WWI fuelled the Russian Revolution and her ascent as the world's first communist state. The First World War helped occupied countries like Poland, Yugoslavia and Hungary to gain their independence but it also set the stage for World War II only a couple decades later. Yet, WWI began almost by accident.

The Serbian & Austro-Hungarian Conflict

There were three great European powers at the start of the 20th century; The Austro-Hungarian, the Russians and the Ottoman Empire.

On June 28th, 1914 in Sarajevo, Serbian Gavrilo Princip, in an act of terrorism, assassinated the heir apparent of the Austro-Hungarian Empire, Archduke Franz Ferdinand.

The Austro-Hungarian Empire contained up to ten different nationalities and kept the peace on the western borders. It was ruled by Franz Ferdinand's uncle, Franz Joseph who had been in power for 66 years.

Serbia had set itself up as an independent state by 1914 and viewed Franz Joseph and the Austro-Hungarian Empire, as the oppressive, undemocratic enemy. Serbia hoped to somehow break up the Austro-Hungarian Empire and opposed any kind of friendship.

Unlike his uncle, Franz Ferdinand believed in political reform. As the Emperor-in-waiting, his ideas were radical. He believed that after decades of oppressive ruling, the existing political system was one that simply could not last. He wanted to avoid war with Serbia and felt that minorities within the empire would look to other countries for help if they didn't have the power to govern themselves within the empire. His vision was to create a new empire called the "United States of Great Austria," in hopes of developing a peaceful co-existence with Serbia.

However, Archduke Franz Ferdinand's decision to visit Sarajevo on June 28th 1914 was ill-conceived in that this was Serbian National Day. Austria-Hungary viewed the assassination as Serbia's declaration of war against Austria-Hungary, achieving the exact opposite of what Franz Ferdinand had hoped for.

WWI Alliances

Serbia's great ally was Russia. The Austro-Hungarian ally was Germany. In its decision to back Austria-Hungary, Germany failed to consider the consequences and neglected to find out exactly what Austria-Hungary was planning. Germany felt that Russian would stay out of the conflict in order to avoid internal revolution. The German Kaiser was so confident that Russia would not want to go to war that he immediately left for vacation.

Declarations of War

The powers of Europe were divided into two main divisions with Germany, Austria-Hungary and Italy comprising one camp and France and Russian making up the other. If Germany backed Austria-Hungary against Serbia and the Russians backed Serbia, then Germany would be forced to go to war against Russia and Russia's ally, France. This is exactly what happened.

- Austria-Hungary declared war on Serbia on July 28th 1914
- Germany declared war on Russia on August 1st
- Germany declared war on France on August 3rd (since France was an ally of Russia)
- Britain declared war on Germany on August 4th (after Germany invaded neutral Belgium)

Britain had initially been asked by Russia to back Russia and France however Britain's decision to enter the war was more out of protecting Britain's global trade and security interests. Britain's empire also extended into colonies in South Africa and India but Britain was not powerful enough to defend her vast empire without the help of France and Russia.

In Europe the neutral countries of Belgium, Poland, Ukraine, Lithuania and Croatia were caught in the middle. In Belgium alone over 11,000,000 people lived under German occupation.
U.S. Enters the War

Throughout the first three years of the war the United States remained neutral even though German submarines had sunk the civilian cruise liner, the Lusitania on May 7th 1915 and bombed the munitions storage docks in New York harbour shortly thereafter.

Throughout the war the United States was supplying munitions and supplies to both the Allies and the Central Powers. In essence, the war was excellent for the American economy. The U.S. joined the Allies on April 6th 1917 only after discovering from British Intelligence that Germany had been secretly encouraging Mexico to declare war on the United States.

A Defensive War

Other than Austria-Hungary's offence against Serbia, the other countries involved in World War One were not fighting an offensive war. Most were convinced that they were fighting a defensive war, one that was forced on them by someone else.

Logistics of a Global War

WWI was a global war that reached beyond the countries of Europe into the Balkans and South Africa. This was a war fought in trenches, in deserts, in mountains, at sea and by air. The vast distances and in many cases the difficult terrain created great challenges to both sides in terms of effective communication, transporting supplies and troops and simply protecting their interests. On the Western Front in France and Belgium, both sides created a series of primitive tunnels that extended for miles underground. Tunnels were used for communications, headquarters, intelligence, dressing posts, etc.

The Christmas Truce—Dec 1914

In December of 1914 soldiers from both sides put down their weapons and met peacefully between the trenches in "no man's land," in a Christmas truce. German and Allied soldiers buried their dead, then shared cigarettes, stories and photos of loved ones. They played soccer, sang Christmas songs and even exchanged gifts until they were forced to return to their trenches by commanding officers.

IN FLANDERS FIELDS—May 1915

The poem IN FLANDERS FIELDS was composed at the battlefront on May 3, 1915 during the second battle of Ypres by Lieutenant Colonel John McCrae, a field surgeon with the Canadian Army Medical Corps. Within months of its first publication in Punch Magazine (December of 1915) IN FLANDERS FIELDS became the most popular poem of the First World War. It is credited as the inspiration behind adopting the red poppy as a symbol of Remembrance and passages were used to further the war efforts, assisting in the sale of over $400,000,000 in war bonds.

Cultures of War

In all there were over 50 different cultures involved in the war. Britain and France deployed troops from every continent and mobilized their colonial empires for the war efforts. The French deployed African soldiers from West and North Africa. Britain mobilized South African troops and soldiers from their colonies in India. The Canadian army included Eskimo and Aboriginal soldiers and New Zealand's army included the indigenous people of the Maori. There were also soldiers from Australia, Pakistan, Spain, Algiers, Scotland and Ireland. Behind the war was an unprecedented workforce of numerous ethnic origins including people from Egypt, Fiji, Vietnam, China and Madagascar. The largest ethnic group, the Chinese Labour Corps, remained in France and Belgium as late as 1919 to help bury the dead and clean up the battlefields.

A New Kind of War—Military Firsts

WWI was the first major war in over 40 years. Both sides had amassed new weapons and technology that had never been used before in actual combat. This was a new kind of war where soldiers were still learning their weapons. It was a war with many "firsts" including the first use of:

- Tanks & Trucks
- Airships & Planes
- Submarines
- Wireless Communication (telegraph)
- Machine Guns
- Long Range Artillery
- Exploding Shells (designed to do as much damage as possible with flying shrapnel)
- Flame Throwers
- Poisonous Gas

WWI Stalemate

Within the first few months of battle in Europe, both sides met with equal opposition, causing both sides to "dig in", creating a series of trenches that ran nearly 450 miles from the coast of Northern Belgium through Northern France to the border of Switzerland. For the next four years WWI on the Western Front (as this area was named) remained at a virtual stalemate, where very little ground was gained by either side. Parallel trenches ran the full length of the battlefront, separated by only a few hundred yards called "no man's land", which was fortified with rolls of barbed wire and heavily shelled throughout the conflict. This was a war without precedent. WWI was the first man-made catastrophe of the 20th century that devastated both sides. There were almost 40 million casualties in total, including nearly ten million military deaths, nearly nine million civilian deaths and just fewer than twenty million military wounded.

WWI Cemeteries and Memorials

Britain's empire was vast and included colonies around the globe including South Africa, India, Australia, New Zealand and Canada. The policy of the British was to bury their war dead where they fell, in the land where they had given their lives to defend. Today the area of the Western Front in France and Belgium contains the graves of hundreds of thousands of WWI soldiers from practically every country involved in the war. Memorials commemorate over 100,000 who went missing in action or could not be identified.

One can chart WWI's progress of devastation and sacrifice simply through the hundreds of cemeteries and memorials that remain. The largest commonwealth cemetery is Tyne Cot Cemetery, which contains nearly 12,000 graves (more than 8000 of those are unidentified) plus a memorial for over 35,000 missing in action. On the memorial headstones of the unknown is the inscription "A SOLDIER OF THE GREAT WAR, KNOWN UNTO GOD". The largest memorial for the missing is Menin Gate in Ypres, Belgium, commemorating 54,896 WWI soldiers with no known graves.

Sinking Morale

At the outbreak of WWI in August of 1914 many thought it would be a short war, and over by Christmas. Fearing they would "miss out" on teaching the Kaiser a lesson, the majority was eager to enlist. There was widespread enthusiasm in anticipation of the new adventures that lay ahead in Europe.

Within a few short months this enthusiasm gave way to the realities of war. Soldiers witnessed the senseless slaughter of hundreds of thousands of their comrades all the while fighting in the most appalling conditions. As the war wore on, the morale of soldiers on both sides deteriorated irrevocably.

WWI—1918 The Final Year

In the latter stage of the war the biggest threat for both sides came not from their enemies but from their civilians and their alliances. Each side remained in a desperate race between winning the war and collapse on the home front.

Alliances Crumble

By the spring of 1918, there was much dissention within the alliances. Austria-Hungary was bankrupt and experiencing widespread famine. Emperor Franz Joseph had died in 1916 and the new ruler, Kaiser Karl opened secret peace negotiations with France in 1917, leaving Germany feeling betrayed. Germany's other ally was the Ottoman-Turkey, but that empire had been in a string of conflicts for more than seven years. The empire was impoverished, crumbling and desperate, which hindered its ability to remain in the war.

By 1918 Russia had all but withdrawn from the war as well, due to the Russian Revolution and eventual civil war. The Russian economy was in ruin and there were great shortages of food and supplies. Russia's military losses were quite heavy totalling nearly 5,000,000 men. By then, most civilians opposed Russia's involvement in the war. Soldiers were ill equipped, morale was at its lowest and many soldiers defected or mutinied.

Germany's Days Are Numbered

The lack of food, morale, supplies and munitions also plagued the Central Powers. This had been a long war with little gains for either side and by 1918 everyone was war-weary. The defeatist attitude of the soldiers and civilians only increased, as did the growing opposition to the war as news of Russia's revolution reached the Western Front. Strikes and rumours of rebellion were not uncommon. Domestic production of munitions and supplies could barely keep up with the demand as raw materials were becoming increasingly difficult to find. Civilians and soldiers wanted change and a return to peace.

The Central Powers were running short on military supplies, and running out of men. Human losses were unprecedented and many new recruits were scarcely trained before being called up for active duty. When Russia pulled out of the war it freed up half a million German soldiers, which temporarily boosted Germany's confidence in its bid to win the war before the Americans arrived.

Germany failed to achieve a decisive victory against the Allies before Americans entered the war. As the Central powers were falling apart the Allies were becoming stronger. The Allies reorganized their command structure and the presence of the Americans gave the Allied troops a huge morale boost. While Germany's numbers were dwindling, America was adding troops to the Allied forces at a rate of 250,000 a month.

The Loss of Bulgaria

By the end of summer in 1918 Germany's troops were fed up, over exhausted and hungry. Since March of that year Germany had lost almost a million men. Those that remained felt they hadn't been given adequate supplies or leadership. The final blow came in September of 1918 with the loss of Bulgaria to the Allies. Bulgaria was Germany's stronghold for the Balkan Front.

Germany Requests Armistice

In early October Germany approached U.S. President Woodrow Wilson requesting that America arbitrate an Armistice between the Central Powers and the Allies. Unfortunately, the war raged on for another six weeks as the politicians argued a peace treaty. The Allies wanted nothing less than to force Germany to surrender unconditionally. Admitting total defeat would make Germany responsible for paying for the costs of war. The closer to Armistice the harder it was to bear the losses, yet some of the fiercest fighting of WWI took place in the last few weeks of the war.

The Kaiser Abdicates

While the Armistice conditions were being handed over to the German officials 45 miles outside of Paris, the people of Germany were rebelling against the Kaiser and screaming for democracy. The Kaiser ordered the military to fire on the civilians and when the military refused the Kaiser was forced to abdicate his power and exiled to Holland shortly thereafter.

Armistice

The ceasefire of the First World War took effect on the 11th hour, of the 11th day of the 11th month of 1918. The war was over. Peace and safety was new and a difficult concept for many to grasp.

From www.flandersfieldsmusic.com/thepoem.html

This was the setting both William and Robert were coming into when they joined the Canadian Forces and made it to in England in August of 1916. The records show the first time they would have fought in the same battle was Ancre Heights, then Vimy Ridge, the third time side-by-side battle in 1917 would have been the Battle of Passchendaele.

In 1918 the 13th and the 46th Battalions teamed up in three more battles: The Battle of Amiens, the Battles of Drocourt-Queant and the Battle of Canal du Nord. In the following pages I have outlined these battles, along with the battle of Valenciennes, where Uncle Will was killed.

Chapter 2

Ancre Heights: 1 Oct-11 Nov 1916

The battle of the Ancre Heights of 1 October-11 November 1916 was part of the wider *first battle of the Somme*. It was fought on the left of the British line of the Somme, with the aim of pinching out a German salient on the Ancre River created by the limited British advances further along the line. The attack was to be launched by the Reserve Army, which held the front on either side of the Ancre.

One attack was to be made on the front north from Hamel, on the right bank of the Ancre. It was hoped that this attack would advance east along a five mile front, and that its right flank would reach Miraumont on the Ancre, then four miles behind the German front line. A second attack would be made on the left back of the river, from the Thiepval Ridge. This attack also had Miraumont as its target. The attack on the Ancre Heights was to be launched at the same time as a Fourth Army attack further east (battle of the Transloy Ridges, 1-18 October 1916).

The main attack was to begin on 12 October (the official battle dates includes the preparation period). *General Gough,* commander of the Reserve Army (to become the Fifth Army at the end of

October), spend the first part of October reorganising his units and launching preparatory attacks.

These included an attack by the Canadian Corps north of Courcelette, on the right flank of the Reserve Army, designed to capture part of the German front line (the Regina Trench) defended by the German Marine Brigade. On 1 October the Canadians advanced 400 yards east of Courcelette, but made no progress against their primary target. At no point did they capture the Regina Trench. Worse, by the end of 17 October they had made very little further progress and were still short of their primary target for 1 October.

Below is Uncle Bob's 13th Bn of the 3rd CDN INF BDE in looking at the map they had the largest stretch of no man's land to cover to reach their objective.

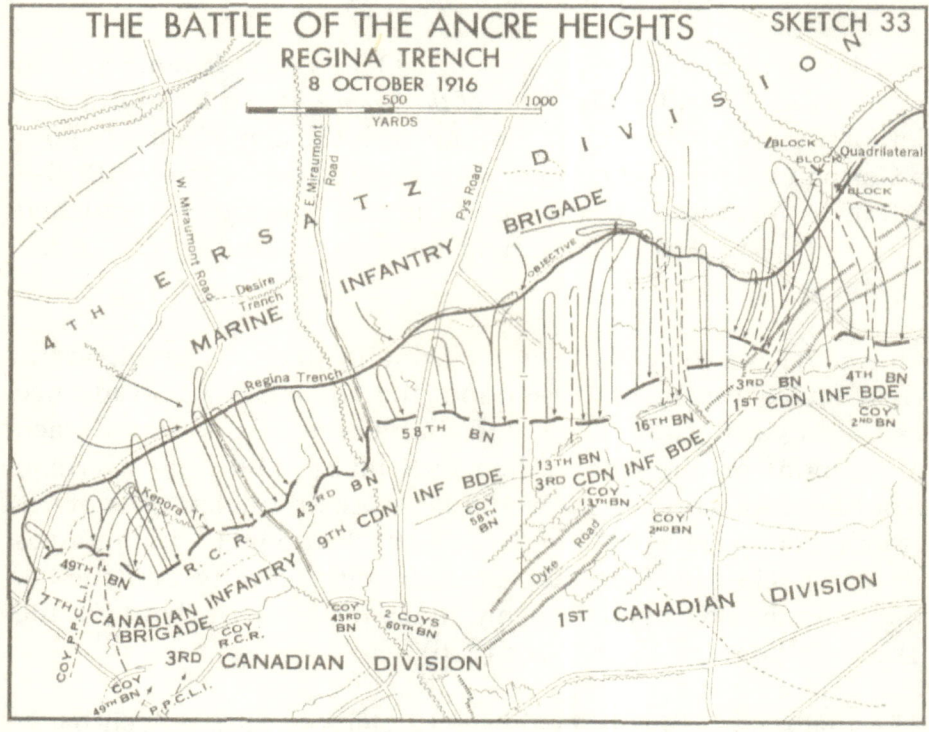

By 12 October, the weather was so bad that the planned offensive had to be postponed. The attack north of the Ancre was cancelled, and a new plan put in place. This involved an attack on the Regina Trench on 21 October, followed by an attack along the Ancre to 25 October.

On 15 October Gough issued orders for the new attack along the Ancre. It would be carried out by II Corps south of the river and V corps to the north. Its objectives included the ridge north of Courcelette, Miraumont, Serre, Pys and Irles, all on the or close to the Ancre. By the end of the entire battle of the Somme the only one of these objectives that would have been achieved was the partial clearance of the Courcelette ridge.

The attack on the Regina Trench went in at 12.06 pm on 21 October, and was a rare success. Supported by 200 heavy guns and howitzers, in half an hour II Corps captured the German front line on a front that ran from Thiepval to Courcelette. Once in the German trenches it was discovered that due to the convex nature of the ground to the north, they did not command a view down into the Ancre valley.

The main attack along the Ancre was repeatedly postponed due to poor weather, first to 1st November, then to 5th November and then indefinitely. Finally a more limited attack along the Ancre was carried out in mid November to pinch out the tip of the German salient on the Ancre.

The battle of the Ancre, 13-19 November 1916, was the final phase of the *first battle of the Somme*. It involved an attack on the German front line as it crossed the Ancre River, a sector of the front that had first been attacked on the first day of the battle without success. The attack along the Ancre had originally been planned for 15 October, as part of the *battle of the Ancre Heights*, but had been postponed repeatedly by bad weather. By November the original plan had been reducing in scope from an attempt to push the Germans back up to five miles along the Ancre to one to capture Beaucourt and push the Germans back at most two miles.

This was a strong sector of the German front. The first British objective involved an advance of 800 yards and would require the capture of at least three lines of trenches. The next target was the German second line, from Serre south to the Ancre. Finally it was hoped to capture Beaucourt, on the Ancre.

The attack would be launched by II Corps south of the river and V Corps to the north, with V Corps carrying out the main offensive. The attack immediately north of the river was to be carried out by the 63rd (R.N.) Division, under Major-General C. D. Shute. This was the first time they had taken part in an attack on the Western Front, and so extra care was taken to make sure everybody knew what was expected of them. Amongst their officers was Lieutenant-Colonel B. C. Freyberg, later to hold high command in the Second World War, who commanded the Hood Battalion (the Naval battalions were named after famous sailors—Hood, Drake, Nelson and Hawke). The division captured the German front line despite heavy German resistance.

Further north the attack made less progress, and so despite Freyberg's optimism the attack on Beaucourt was delayed until the next day. 51st Division captured Beaumont Hamel, and 2nd Division managed to capture parts of Redan Ridge, but further north no progress was made.

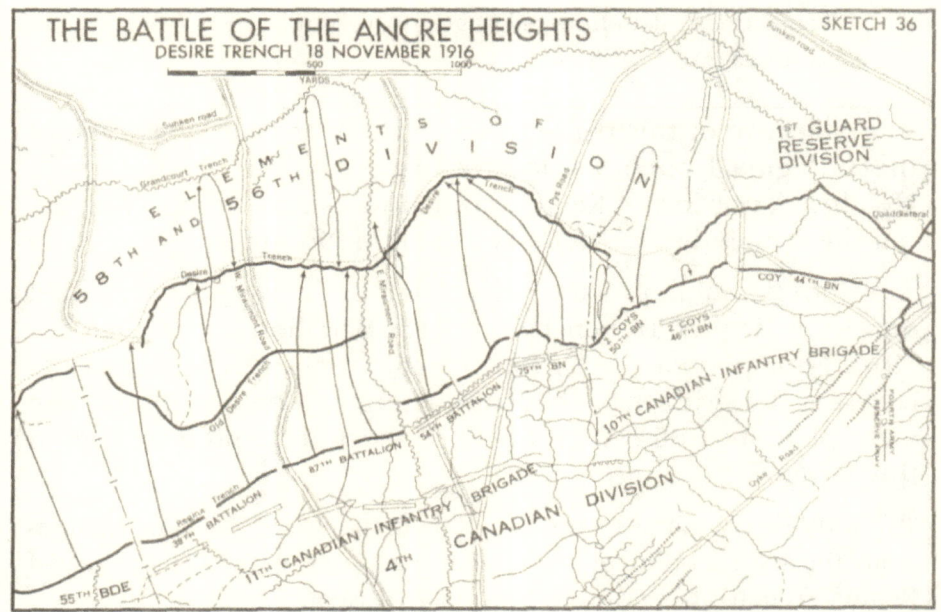

The attack was renewed on 14 November. This time the 63rd Division was able to secure Beaucourt, which fell at 10.30am. The success at Beaucourt encouraged Gough to plan for a more ambitious offensive, but Haig ordered him to wait until after he could return from the Chantilly Conference of 15-16 November.

One final attack was made, on 18-19 November. This began in snow and sleet and descended into chaos. On the right of the line the 4th Canadian Division captured its first objectives, but elsewhere little was achieved.

The attack was a relative success. Beaumont Hamel and Beaucourt were captured, but Serre and the northern part of the German line remained untouched. Once again mud intervened to help the defenders, preventing the use of the few available tanks, and making all communication difficult. All the early successes on the Ancre achieved was the creation of a British held salient on the Ancre, which proved to be a very dangerous area to be posted over the winter of 1916-17.

From the Saskatchewan Dragoons website, http://www.
saskd.ca/skd-hon.htm

The objective of this battle was a series of trench lines. One of
these, Regina Trench, was located just behind the crest of Ancre
Heights. A portion of Regina Trench was siezed on 21 October,
but the remainder was not taken until 11 November.

The 46th Battalion provided eight platoons in support of a failed
attack on Regina Trench by the 44th Battalion on 25 October
1916. Four platoons, with four machine guns, were to provide
covering fire, with the other four acting as a digging party. The
eight platoons suffered 14 killed, 36 wounded, and 2 missing in
this action.

"B" and "C" companies from the 46th Battalion, and two companies
from the 47th, conducted an attack on 11 November which seized
Regina Trench, at a cost to the 46th of 81 casualties

Chapter 3 — Vimy Ridge

Preparing for the attack of Vimy Ridge

No Allied operation on the Western Front was more thoroughly planned than this deliberate frontal attack on what seemed to be virtually invincible positions. Vimy Ridge was so well fortified that all previous attempts to capture it had failed. However, Canadian

Figure 7 Picture of Vimy Ridge

commanders had learned bitter lessons from the cost of past frontal assaults made by vulnerable infantry. This time their preparations were elaborate. As the Canadian Commander of Uncle Bob's, 1st Division, Major-General Arthur Currie, said, "Take time to train them." This is exactly what the Canadian Corps did, down to the smallest unit and the individual soldier.

In the late autumn of 1916, the Canadians moved north, capping their ordeal on the Somme, to relieve British troops opposite the western slopes of Vimy Ridge. They spent the coldest winter of the war strengthening defences, carrying out increasingly frequent raids on enemy trenches and gathering intelligence, in preparation for the spring offensive. Continual raiding from mid-March on cost the Canadians 1,400 casualties. However, the knowledge gained would later help the Canadians take their Vimy objectives with lighter losses.

A full-scale replica of the battle area was laid out with reams of coloured tape and flags behind the Canadian lines. Here Canadian units carried out repeated exercises, rehearsing exactly what they would do throughout the day of the attack. Maps were given out to guide the smallest units. The troops were fully informed about their objectives and their routes.

Military mining had long been a feature of war on Vimy Ridge. German, French and British engineers had dug many long tunnels under No Man's Land. They filled them with explosive charges, which blew up enemy trenches, leaving huge craters as new features of the landscape. Working at night, tunnelling companies used the existing tunnels to build a new underground network for the Vimy assault. As well, they dug 12 deep subways, totalling more than five kilometres in length, through which assault troops could move to their jumping-off points. The subways protected them from shelling and permitted the wounded to be brought back from the battlefield. Some subways were quite short, while one, the Goodman Subway, opposite La Folie Farm, was 1.2 kilometres long. All had piped water and most were lit by electricity provided by generators. They also housed telephone lines.

Into the walls of the subways were cut chambers for brigade and battalion headquarters, ammunition stores, communications centres and dressing stations. The largest of several deep caverns, the Zivy Cave could hold a whole battalion.

Smaller tunnels leading off the subways to the front line—saps they were called (the title, sapper, meaning military engineer or engineer private, derives from this term)—were sealed until Zero Hour and then blown out. At that point, the Canadians would push out to attack, right onto the battlefield.

The maze of tunnels and caverns was one of the most remarkable engineering feats of the war. The extensive underground network would reduce casualties amongst the advancing infantry and returning wounded, and enable supplies to be brought up under less hazardous conditions.

In addition to constructing this network, Canadian and British engineers repaired 40 kilometres of road in the Corps' forward area and added 4.8 kilometres of new plank road. They also reconditioned 32 kilometres of tramways, over which light trains, hauled by gasoline engines or mules, carried stores and ammunition.

The infantry assault was preceded by a massive artillery barrage, which began on March 20. This involved 245 heavy guns and howitzers, and more than 600 pieces of field artillery. Supporting British artillery added 132 more heavy guns and 102 field pieces. All this firepower amounted to one heavy gun for every 20 metres of frontage and one field gun for every 10 metres.

On April 2, the bombardment was stepped up. By the time the infantry set out, a million artillery shells had battered the Germans. One Canadian commented that shells poured over his head onto enemy positions "like water from a hose". More than 80 per cent of the German guns had been identified by aerial reconnaissance and by other spotting methods which Canadians had perfected. Few survived intact. The Germans called the period "the week of suffering." Trenches were shattered and a new artillery shell-fuse demolished many barbed-wire entanglements, thereby easing the Canadians' dangerous path to combat.

The impact of the air war was significant at Vimy. While aerial reconnaissance yielded valuable intelligence about enemy positions and artillery sites, fighter aircraft prevented the enemy from gaining a clear idea of Allied intentions. German observation aircraft and balloons were attacked and shot down. This work was important and dangerous—balloons were defended by fighters and anti-aircraft guns. The soon-to-be-famous Canadian fighter pilot, Billy Bishop, won the Military Cross on April 7 for shooting down a balloon near Vimy. He had begun his remarkable career in March.

The Capture of Vimy Ridge

At 5.30 a.m., April 9, 1917, Easter Monday, the creeping artillery barrage began to move steadily toward the Germans. Behind it advanced 20,000 soldiers of the first attacking wave of the four Canadian divisions, a score of battalions in line abreast, leading the assault in a driving north-west wind that swept the mangled countryside with sleet and snow. Guided by paint-marked stakes, the leading infantry companies crossed the devastation of No Man's Land, picking their way through shell-holes and shattered trenches. They were heavily laden. Each soldier carried at least 32 kilograms of equipment, plus, some say, a similar weight of the all-pervasive mud on uniform and equipment. This burden made climbing in and out of the numerous trenches and craters particularly difficult.

There was some hand-to-hand fighting, but the greatest resistance, and heavy Canadian losses, came from the strongly-emplaced machine-guns in the German intermediate line. Overcoming this resistance, three of the four divisions captured their part of the Ridge by midday, right on schedule. In the final stage, the 2nd Canadian Division was assisted by the British 13th Brigade, which fell under its command for the operation.

Uncle Will's, 4th Canadian Division's principal objective was Hill 145, the highest and most important feature of the whole Ridge. Once taken, its summit would give the Canadians a commanding view of German rearward defences in the Douai Plain as well as those remaining on the Ridge itself.

Because of its importance, the Germans had fortified Hill 145 with well-wired trenches and a series of deep dug-outs beneath its rear slope. The brigades of the 4th Division were hampered by fire from the Pimple, the other prominent height, which inflicted costly losses on the advancing waves of infantry. Renewed attacks were mounted using troops that were originally scheduled to attack the Pimple. Finally, in the afternoon of April 10, a fresh assault by a relieving brigade cleared the summit of Hill 145 and thus placed the whole of Vimy Ridge in Canadian hands. Two days later, units of the Uncle Will's, 10th Canadian Brigade successfully stormed the Pimple. By that time, the enemy had accepted the loss of Vimy Ridge as permanent and had pulled back more than three kilometres.

Vimy Ridge marked the only significant success of the Allied spring offensive of 1917. But though they had won a great tactical victory, the Canadians were unable to exploit their success quickly with a breakthrough, mainly because their artillery had bogged down and was unable to move up with them through the muddy, shell-torn ground. Instead, some Canadian artillerymen took over captured German guns which they had earlier been trained to fire.

The Canadian achievement in capturing Vimy Ridge owed its success to sound and meticulous planning and thorough preparation, all of which was aimed at minimizing casualties. But it was the splendid fighting qualities and devotion to duty of Canadian officers and soldiers on the battlefield that were decisive. Most of them citizen-soldiers, they performed like professionals.

Canadians attacked German machine-guns, the greatest obstacles to their advance, with great courage. They saved many comrades' lives as a result. Four won the Victoria Cross for their bravery in such dangerous exploits. Of these, three were earned on the opening day of the battle.

Private William Milne of the 16th Battalion won the VC when he crawled up to a German machine-gun that had been firing on the advancing Canadians, bombed its crew and captured the gun. Later, he stalked a second machine-gun, killing its crew and capturing it, but was himself killed shortly thereafter. The whereabouts of Private Milne's grave is unknown.

Lance-Sergeant Ellis Sifton of the 18th Battalion charged a machine-gun post single-handed, leaping into the trench where it was concealed and killing its crew. Soon after, he was met by a small party of Germans who were advancing through the trench. He managed to hold them off until his comrades arrived, but then one of his victims, gasping a last breath of life, fired upon him.

During the fight for Hill 145, Captain Thain MacDowell of the 38th Battalion entered an enemy dug-out, where he tricked 77 Prussian Guards into surrendering and captured two machine-guns by pretending he had a large force behind him. His large force consisted of two soldiers. MacDowell had earned the Distinguished Service Order on the Somme.

On April 10, Private John Pattison of the 50th Battalion jumped from shell-hole to shell-hole until, 30 metres from an enemy machine-gun, he was in range to bomb its crew. He then rushed forward to bayonet the remaining five gunners. Pattison was killed two months later.

Of the four Vimy VCs, only Captain MacDowell survived the War.

At Vimy, the Canadian Corps had captured more ground, more prisoners and more guns than any previous British offensive in two-and-a-half years of war. It was one of the most complete and decisive engagements of the Great War and the greatest Allied victory up to that time. The Canadians had demonstrated they were one of the outstanding formations on the Western Front and masters of offensive warfare.

Though the victory at Vimy came swiftly, it did not come without cost. There were 3,598 dead out of 10,602 Canadian casualties. Battalions in the first waves of the assault suffered grievously. No level of casualties could ever be called acceptable, but those at Vimy were lower than the terrible norm of many major assaults on the Western Front. They were also far lighter than those of any previous offensive at the Ridge. Earlier French, British and German struggles there had cost at least 200,000 casualties. Care in planning by the Corps Commander, Sir Julian Byng, and his right-hand man, Arthur Currie, kept Canadian casualties down.

The Canadian success at Vimy marked a profound turning-point for the Allies. A year-and-a-half later, the Great War was over. The

Canadian record, crowned by the achievements at Vimy, won for Canada a separate signature on the Versailles Peace Treaty ending the war. Back home, the victory at Vimy, won by troops from every part of the country, helped unite many Canadians in pride at the courage of their citizen-soldiers, and established a feeling of real nationhood.

Brigadier-General Alexander Ross had commanded the 28th (North-West) Battalion at Vimy. Later, as president of the Canadian Legion, he proposed the first Veterans' post-war, pilgrimage to the new Vimy Memorial in 1936. He said of the battle:

"It was Canada from the Atlantic to the Pacific on parade. I thought then . . . that in those few minutes I witnessed the birth of a nation."

From Veterans Affairs Canadawww.vac-acc.gc.ca/remembers

From the Saskatchewan Dragoons website,http://www. saskd.ca/skd-hon.htm

The strong German defences on Vimy Ridge had easily beaten back all previous assaults. Now the newly-formed Canadian Corps, consisting of all four Canadian divisions under the command of British General (and future Governor General of Canada) Julian Byng, was given the task of taking the ridge. On the morning of 9 April, Easter Monday, the Canadian Corps stormed up Vimy Ridge through a driving snowstorm in a meticulously-planned assault, and captured most of the position. By the 12th, Vimy Ridge was entirely in Canadian hands. On the 13th, Canadian soldiers moved virtually unopposed down the other side of the ridge and through the villages of Angres and Givenchy; the loss of Vimy Ridge had forced the Germans to pull back.

The 46th Battalion (codenamed "Harland") started the battle in reserve. However, A and B Companies moved up and onto the attack on the first day, with B Company taking three large craters near Hill 145, and A Company extending the line from there to make contact with the 11th Brigade on their right. On 10 April, the two companies, reinforced with a platoon from C Company, were attached to the 44th and 50th Battalions for the successful assault on Hill 145, the highest point on Vimy Ridge.

On 12 April, C and D Companies and the 50th and 44th Battalions stormed The Pimple and took it away from the Prussian 5th Guard Grenadier Regiment. The two companies took part in the advance through Givenchy on 13 April, and were relieved by the 1st Duke of Cornwall's Light Infantry east of Givenchy on 14 April. The 46th Battalion suffered 67 killed, 157 wounded, and several missing in the battle for Vimy Ridge.

"Am sending you with bearer (your own Company runner) the following reinforcements:

1 NCO and 6 men, also 3 L.A.R.[1] men who will reinforce Lt. Johnson's post. These are carrying some bombs[2] and R.[3] Grenades. Also flares and white tape. Also 8 one-gallon jars rum."

> Message from the Commanding Officer of the 46th Battalion to the Officer Commanding "C" Company, 3:20 pm, 12 April 1917.

[1] Lewis Automatic Rifle, a light machine gun better known as the Lewis gun.
[2] Hand grenades
[3] Rifle grenades

Chapter 4

PASSCHENDAELE—(October and November, 1917)

"... I died in Hell

(they called it Passchendaele)
my wound was slight and I was
hobbling back; and then a shell
burst slick upon the duckboards;
so I fell into the bottomless mud,
and lost the light"

... Siegfried Sassoon

Figure 8 Passchendaele Tranches

When one ponders the waste, stupidity, mud and gross loss of human life during the Great War, it is usually the battle of Passchendaele that comes to mind. This brainchild of Field Marshal Douglas Haig—also called The Third Battle of Ypres—officially began on July 31, 1917. Examining the general objectives, I guess it is possible to view the initial assault as worth attempting. It was hoped that smashing the German lines at Flanders would allow the allies to break through to the coastal ports of Belgium, causing considerable damage to the U-Boat offensive of Germany, as well as, causing serious damage to the German defensive strategy on their Belgian flank. The blundering and inexcusable waste of lives comes into play as it become obvious that Haig is willing to continue on with a poor plan regardless of weather conditions and German opposition. The full level of his poor leadership is seen when viewing the results: a gain of little importance with tremendous loss of life.

Four million shells were used to "soften-up" the German defences as the attack began with a resulting destruction of the water table and drainage system of this lowland region. Streams and creeks were obliterated. The attack commenced at the same time the seasonal rains hit the region. Men and tanks had huge difficulty moving on the field of battle. Artillery could not hold positions properly as the footings were placed on the soggy ground. German defences had taken on a strategy of housing the men in concrete "pill boxes" on the slightly higher ground of the ridge giving their machine guns cover and an open field of fire to destroy the attacking forces. As the men strayed onto the battlefield, it was soon obvious that success would be almost impossible and slaughter guaranteed. Men who had the misfortune of falling from the duckboard walkways faced a death of drowning in the mud of the shell holes. As the summer worked itself into early fall, it was obvious that no great breakthrough was to happen and that the British forces would face a gradual reduction in their numbers, morale and chances for victory.

By October of 1917, the Canadian troops were called upon to enter the situation and bring about a successful conclusion to this disaster. It was hoped that not only would the battle be turned in favour of the allies but also, unofficially of course, save the career of Field Marshal Haig. By the time the Canadians arrived at Passchendaele practically no objectives had been met. General Currie, Commander of the Canadian Corps, wanted no part of this enterprise but was soundly over-ruled by the British High Command. In fact, they were prepared to send their most innovative and gifted officer packing if he showed any more resistance to the order. Currie did, however, manage to win the point that extensive preparations and planning would be needed and that time must be granted for the Canadians to prepare and hopefully avoid making the same errors that had caused so much suffering for the British and Australian forces.

The field as faced by the Canadians was full of mud, water, corpses, dead horses, barbed wire and miscellaneous wreckage of almost four months of battle. The trench lines were almost unrecognizable due to the water and mud. The Canadian plan began with the rebuilding of the transport systems and an attempt to drain the field as best as possible. German shelling, aircraft attacks and nature caused over 1500 Canadian casualties before the attack even started.

The Canadians attacked on October 26, 1917 behind a covering artillery assault. Movement would be in small steps rather than great frontal assaults on German lines. Gradual steps into German positions would be accomplished to cover each successive move of the troops. Fresh reserve troops would come into position within two days to spell those on the front lines. The first day saw almost 2500 casualties. The next bite into the German lines would be on October 30 following an even larger artillery assault. German concrete bunkers would be destroyed by the artillery—not through direct hits—which did little, but often by destroying the ground surrounding them and causing the footings to shift. Should this fail, the bravery of the men would prove to be a success. This strategy of taking steps to reach the objective was working but costly. By November 10 the ridge had fallen to the Canadians. The Germans were ordered to retake the position at all costs but could not.

By November 14, 1917 the Canadians, having done what was asked of them, retired back to the Vimy region. Their positions were taken up by British troops. Almost 15,654 Canadian casualties had been counted (Currie had warned the British High Command that victory would cause 16,000 casualties a month earlier). Nine Canadians had earned the Victoria Cross. Roughly two square miles had been taken at a cost of 500,000 casualties to the Allied forces. Field Marshall Haig was spared his career.

With little fanfare and a grudging recognition of their deeds, the Canadian Corps had proven to all that their bravery, planning, training and skill had made them the elite Corps of the allied forces. With this killing ground behind them, the Canadians would take up their positions by Arras / Vimy / Lens and prepare to take on the final German defences of the Siegfried Line and in fact, lead the final assault that would bring the war to a close.

The Canadian Corps carried through the assault for the "symbolic smear of brick" that was Paaschendaele, fighting in soupy mud against Germans emplaced in concrete bunkers. The Corps achieved its objective at a cost only fractionally less than LGen Currie's pre-battle estimate of 16,000 (**80%**) casualties. Within six months, the ground they had won was retaken by the Germans.

From the Saskatchewan Dragoons website,
http://www.saskd.ca/skd-hon.htm

The 46th Battalion attacked at dawn on 26 October with four companies, each having four officers and about 131 other ranks. Attacking on a three-company front, with B Company in reserve, they reached their objectives by about 8 am. The cost was frightful, with many casualties caused by shells from the covering barrage; the Allied guns, slowly settling in the mud, were firing short. A Company reached its objective with three officers and 71 other ranks; C Company, with a captain and 35 other ranks; and D Company, with 30 other ranks led by a lance-corporal. B Company immediately reinforced the positions, while two officers were brought up from headquarters to take over what was left of D Company. Shortly after 4 pm, the Germans counterattacked. With no artillery support, and with their weapons jamming in the mud, the 46th somehow held their positions long enough for stretcher parties to evacuate the wounded; then they withdrew to the new support trenches dug by elements of the 50th Battalion that day. However, on seeing the 46th pulling back, the 50th withdrew as well, and the 46th continued to fall back to the original jumping-off trenches, where they established a line. There they were reinforced by returning stretcher parties, as well as runners, signallers, orderly room staff and batmen from battalion headquarters, and a company of the 47th Battalion that happened to be nearby. This force advanced and established themselves in the new support trenches. They held these positions until relieved that evening by companies of the 47th Battalion.

The 46th Battalion took 402 casualties that day, of whom 62 were recorded as "missing"—many dead or wounded soldiers simply sank into the mud. Reduced to the equivalent of a single understrength company, the 46th took no further part in the battle. After two days spent recovering the wounded and burying the dead, the battalion was withdrawn to Brandhoek.

"Good God, did we really send men to fight in that?"

Lieutenant-General Sir Launcelot Kiggel, 17 November 1917

"I can forgive the Somme, but I cannot forgive Passchendaele, because the same mistakes were made over again, in a more exaggerated form, and Passchendaele had no value strategically in the over-all picture of the war . . . You don't fight where you are not going to win. And that was not a place to win."

General Frank Worthington

General Worthington, founder of the Royal Canadian Armoured Corps, served at Passchendaele as a private with the Canadian Machine Gun Corp

Chapter 5

Battle of Amiens: 8-11 August 1918

Fourth Army's colossal surprise attack east of Amiens on 8 August, spearheaded by tanks and Canadian and Australian infantry, began with spectacular success(1); but the lavish scale of achievements could not be maintained and during the subsequent three days' fighting forward impetus

Figure 9 Battle of Amiens

slowed. Facing increasingly difficult ground, defended by a reinforced enemy, the faltering rate of advance induced Haig to break off costly British assaults in favour of potentially more rewarding offensive operations on other fronts.

High tank casualties on the previous day meant that significantly fewer vehicles(2) supported the renewed attacks(3) on 9 August, which despite the early capture of Le Quesnel(4), were delayed and disjointed(5) and failed to exploit the opportunities offered by an enemy in full retreat. By nightfall the important Chipilly spur(6) had been secured and a general advance of around three miles achieved.

10 August(7), a fine summer's day, saw French advances on the extreme right of the battlefront (extended by the participation of the French Third Army), but poor communications(8) and command anxieties about German counter-attacks (which effectively shackled the leading Dominion troops) constrained the British advance. Tank casualties(9) were again high as German field gunners took the measure of British armour; Fourth Army's maximum advance, in the Canadian sector, amounted to around two miles. This small progress(10) convinced Haig of the need to switch the fronts(11) of attack.

The good weather continued on 11 August, a day of minimal gains for Fourth Army as Rawlinson sought to conserve his tiring troops; a mere 38 tanks supported a much-restricted advance (including the Australian occupation of Lihons) as the re-organised German defence offered increasingly fierce resistance.

Though huge gains (12) had been made in the four days' fighting, offensive operations were now wound down as preparations began for a major British thrust north of Albert.

Notes

(1) 'Spectacular success'

Thursday 8 August represented a memorable Allied victory—and one which shook to the core the German High Command; for the enthusiastic Allied participants the unprecedented extent of the advance and numbers of prisoners taken seemed to

Figure 10 Spectacular success—'Disenchantment'

signify that a crucial moment in the war had been reached: some
hint of this excitement and sense of exaltation may be seen in C
E Montague's vivid celebration of the achievements of the day:
'Beyond the river a miracle—the miracle—had begun. It was going on fast. Remember that all previous advances had gained us
little more than freedom to skulk up communications trenches
a mile or two further eastward, if that. But now! Across the level
Santerre, which the sun was beginning to fill with mist-filtered lus-
tre, two endless columns of British guns, wagons and troops were
marching steadily east, unshelled over ground that the Germans
had held until dawn. Nothing like it had been seen in the war . . .
Far off, six thousand yards off in the shining south-east, tanks and
cavalry were at work . . . Nearer, the glass could make out an enemy battery, captured complete, caught with the leather caps still
on the muzzle of guns. The British dead on the plain, horses and
men, lay scattered thinly over wide spaces; scarcely a foundered
tank could be seen; the ground had turf on it still; it was only
speckled with shell-holes, not disembowelled or flayed.'

> *Spectacular success*—('Disenchantment', C E Montague,
> London, Chatto & Windus, 1922, pp.174-175).

(2) 'fewer vehicles'

Only 145 out of 415 were available for action next day.More
recent research on Tank Corps records and Fourth Army papers
by Dr Paul Harris has led to a revision of Edmonds' figure: it is
now estimated that the total number of fighting tanks available to
Fourth Army on the morning of 9 August was 155 vehicles. There
is no dispute as regards the acute state of exhaustion (morale and
physical) felt by many of the surviving tank crews as a consequence
of furnace-like conditions experienced within their vehicles and
the intensity of fire they were exposed to; the rate of attrition for
tanks increased on 10 and 11 August; by the 12 August it has been
claimed only six tanks remained fit for action.

> **fewer vehicles'**—('Military Operations. France and
> Belgium, 1918' (Volume IV), compiled by Brigadier-
> General Sir James E Edmonds, London, HMSO, 1947,

p.83, f.n.1). (See: 'Amiens to the Armistice. The BEF in the Hundred Days' Campaign, 8 August-11 November 1918', J P Harris (with Niall Barr), London, Brasseys, 1998, pp.111 and f.n.46). (See: 'Chronicles of the Great War. The Western Front 1914-1918', Peter Simkins, Godalming, Surrey, Bramley Books, 1997, p.204).

(3) 'renewed attacks'

Having secured the Old Amiens Outer Defence Line on the afternoon of 8 August (and with many German ammunition dumps ablaze in the distance), Rawlinson's intention for Fourth Army, despite his concerns of possible German counter-attacks (based on previous experience and a practical assessment of increasing numbers of German reserves being fed into the battle-zone), was 'to advance and establish itself on the general line Roye-Chaulnes-Bray sur Somme-Dernancourt, whilst the French came up to Roye'. This line would require a general Allied advance of seven miles. Throughout the period of the renewed attacks (9-11 August) Allied airpower sought in vain to destroy the Somme bridges behind the active German defence line; another 45 RAF aircraft were lost on 9 August in operations against these targets.

> **'renewed attacks'**—('Military Operations. France and Belgium, 1918' (Volume IV), compiled by Brigadier-General Sir James E Edmonds, London, HMSO, 1947, p.95).

(4) 'capture of Le Quesnel'

The village, which had held out against all attacks on the previous day, was captured as a result of the joint work of 75th and 87th Canadian Battalions (11th Canadian Brigade, 4th Canadian Division) assisted by Brutinel's 'Independent Force': 'Advancing rapidly, by 5.30am the [75th] battalion was in the village and after mopping it up, capturing in the process the effects of a divisional headquarters, continued on. Some severe fighting took place in the wood south of the village . . . It was soon discovered that one pocket of Germans had been left between the two battalions, and another north of le Quesnel. These were dealt with by bombers and with the help of five tanks of the 1st Tank Battalion which remained fit for action, but two of these tanks were now destroyed by an anti-tank gun.

> 'capture of Le Quesnel'' ('Military Operations. France and Belgium, 1918' (Volume IV), compiled by Brigadier-General Sir James E Edmonds, London, HMSO, 1947,

(5) 'delayed and disjointed'

The long delay in offensive activity that followed the capture of Le Quesnel in the early morning of 9 August resulted from the confusion produced by the late changes in operational orders (amended the previous evening). Thus the Canadian Corps' main attack on 9 August began in fits and starts between late morning and 1pm; the Australians too attacked late (around 11am) with varying degrees of tank and artillery support. 'The ground fighting during the day was of a very disjointed nature; the attacks of various divisions and brigades started at different times and under different conditions. Some of them were covered by artillery, some supported by tanks whilst others were carried out by infantry unaided . . . In the result only a bare three-miles advance, half the way to Roye-Chaulnes, was accomplished.

> 'delayed and disjointed'—' ('Military Operations. France and Belgium, 1918' (Volume IV), compiled by Brigadier-General Sir James E Edmonds, London, HMSO, 1947, p.95).

(6) 'Chipilly spur'

The American 131st Regiment (attached to British 58th Division, III Corps) contributed greatly, and with much valour and enthusiasm, to the capture of the heavily defended Chipilly positions: 'Chipilly and Chipilly spur . . . localities formed a little fortress. The spur, extending into an acute southern bend of the Somme rises steeply on its southern and eastern sides from the marshes of the river, whilst its western side is protected by a narrow valley flanked by machine guns which fired up it from Chipilly village and down it from the shelter of Gressaire Wood. Along the path which ran northward from Chipilly below the western edge of the spur was a line of machine guns in concrete emplacements, and a second line was sited on the eastern edge of the spur. Field guns in this village commanded the river bridge and the road approaches from the west.' Despite III Corps good progress on 9 August (during which British units took almost 3,000 prisoners and many guns) it still lagged behind the line of the Australian Corps.

(7) '10 August'

'The achievements of the 10th were disappointing: the various attacks, as on the 9th, started at different times without co-ordination, on the misunderstanding that the operation was a pursuit, whereas German resistance was stiffening. The advance was small, a maximum of a little over two miles on the Canadian Corps front. The French did slightly better than on the 9th, bringing into action on the right of the 1st Army seven divisions of their 3rd Army, thus extending the line of battle by ten miles; the 1st Army occupied Montdidier . . . and as a whole came up nearly abreast of the Canadian Corps. Thus the battle front was increased to 35 miles, from the French right at Chevincourt to the British left at Dernancourt, though as it was slightly concave, its actual length was more. But, like the British, the French advance came to an end when it reached the new German position of resistance.

'10 August'—(Volume IV), compiled by Brigadier-General Sir James E Edmonds, London, HMSO, 1947, p.119).

(8) 'poor communications'

A significant factor affecting the advance and move into 'semi-open warfare' (an unfamiliar experience for all attacking troops in 1918) was the temporary breakdown in the established communications systems—which resulted in frustrating delays and uncertainties: 'Difficulties of communication, now that the trench-warfare telephone system had been left behind, were harassing not only the higher but also the smaller formations, and were to continue to be so in the semi-open warfare that was to follow. In spite of the exertions of the Signal Service, relay chains of runners, cyclists and horsemen established in some divisions could not compete in time and reliability with wires and cables, and when telephone lines were available it was forbidden to use them for operation orders or important messages for fear of being overheard by the enemy.

> **'poor communications'**—(Volume IV), compiled by Brigadier-General Sir James E Edmonds

(9) 'Tank casualties'

Tank casualties were high for the entire period of the battle and despite post-war German claims of their dramatic effectiveness at Amiens (particularly as a demoraliser of infantry), the British Official Historian remained unconvinced of the vehicles' decisive influence: 'The action of the tanks and the cavalry, though they won small triumphs, did not come up to expectation . . . They certainly saved many infantry lives and enabled the attack to go forward more quickly than it would have done without them . . . It should be noticed that the percentage of tanks which were knocked out increased with each day, as the enemy artillery grew accustomed to them: it has been put at 25 per cent on the 8th, 30 per cent on the 9th and 50 per cent on the 10th. It is also now agreed that the 'faster' Whippet tanks' collaboration with cavalry failed to yield the hoped for results: the Whippets were unable to keep up with cavalry units and might better have been employed as agents for deep raiding on the German rear areas.

> **'Tank casualties'**—(The actual performance of the Whippet tank belied its name: with a road speed of 8.3 m.p.h. the 'Medium Mark A' (as the 'Whippet' was more formally known) was no match for cavalry even over the best ground; it was however considerably quicker than the first four Marks of tank used between 1916 and 1917 (3.5 m.p.h.) and the Mark V (4.6 m.p.h.) introduced in 1918).

(10) 'small progress'

The British Official Historian went to some lengths to point out the difficulties posed to the attackers by the topography of the old battlegrounds that they were now approaching: 'The principal reason for this small success was that just ahead of the two French Armies, the Canadian Corps and the right of the Australian Corps lay the remains of the old Allied and German front lines of February 1917, prior to the enemy's retirement to the Hindenburg Line. For a breadth of three miles the ground was pitted with shell holes and intersected by old trenches and belts of wire almost intact and hidden by long grass. These formed a physical obstacle to rapid advance and offered ideal positions to determined machine gunners. The delays of the 9th had enabled the Germans to bring up more reinforcements.

> **'small progress'**—(Volume IV), compiled by Brigadier-General Sir James E Edmonds, London, HMSO, 1947, p.120).

(11) 'switch the fronts'

The problems inherent in 'coalition warfare' again came to the fore on Saturday morning (10 August) after Haig had sent a message to General Horne (Commander of the British First Army) to put in place existing plans for offensive moves in the direction of La Bassée and Aubers ridge 'in conjunction with an advance by the Third Army against Bapaume and the Second Army against Kemmel.' These instructions, which would effectively signify the end of British participation in the Amiens attack displeased Generalissimo Foch who was all for carrying on and expanding the existing eastward and south-eastward thrusts. Haig and Foch met that same day and Haig's clearly stated intention of making Third Army's attack against the German right flank his main priority became the source of considerable friction between the two leaders before a compromise in priorities was formally agreed several days late.

'switch the fronts'—' ('Military Operations. France and Belgium, 1918' (Volume IV), compiled by Brigadier-General Sir James E Edmonds, London, HMSO, 1947, p.133).

(12)   'huge gains'

Between 6 and 15 August 'The French had captured 259 officers and 11,114 other ranks and 259 guns and the British, 439 officers and 18,061 other ranks and 240 guns ... a total of 29,873 prisoners. The British casualties were about 20,000 for the four days of battle, and those of the French First and Third Armies for ten days (6th to 15th August) 24, 232.' ('Military Operations. France and Belgium, The British Official Historian also offered a more precise summary breakdown of Fourth Army casualties (killed, wounded and missing): Cavalry Corps: 887; III Corps: 6,250; Canadian Corps: 9,074; Australian Corps: 5,991. Total casualties were calculated as 22,202 (which included 3,885 killed).

'huge gains'—(6th to 15th August) 24, 232.' ('Military Operations. France and Belgium, 1918' (Volume IV), compiled by Brigadier-General Sir James E Edmonds, London, HMSO, 1947, pp.154-155). (See: 'Military Operations. France and Belgium, 1918' (Volume IV), compiled by Brigadier-General Sir James E Edmonds, London, HMSO, 1947, pp.158-160).

The Australians, supported by large numbers of tanks, were ordered to attack the salient at Amiens created by the German Spring Offensive of 1918. Field Marshal Haig granted the Australians' request that the Canadian Corps fight on their flank. The Canadian Corps moved to the sector in secret, meanwhile sending two battalions, some of its medical units, and all of its radios to Ypres to deceive the Germans, who prepared for an attack wherever Canadian troops appeared. The attack at Amiens took the Germans by surprise. The Canadian Corps advanced eight miles that day and the Australians seven; Field Marshall Ludendorff of the German High Command referred to August 8 as "the black day of the German Army." Although the Canadians advanced another six miles in the next three days, the attack bogged down in the old trench lines of the 1916 battle of the Somme, against German reinforcements, and the battle ended. However, German morale had been severely damaged. This was the turning point of the war.

> From the Saskatchewan Dragoons website, *http://www. saskd.ca/skd-hon.htm*

Elements of the 46th Battalion rode on tanks on the first day of the offensive. The rest of the 46th attacked on 10 August and took the long-abandoned trench lines from the 1916 Battle of the Somme near Maucourt, as well as the village itself. The unit suffered 114 casualties in the action.

The 46th moved back to the support lines on 13 August. On that day their commanding officer, LCol H.J. Dawson, who had contracted influenza but remained with the unit through the battle, collapsed in his dugout and was evacuated as a stretcher case. Under the acting command of Maj J.A. Hope, the battalion relieved the 50th in the front line on the 20th. After being relieved by the 2nd Battalion, 144th French Infantry Regiment on 23 August, they moved to Arras, arriving on the 28th.

Chapter 6

The Battle of the Canal du Nord—
September 27-October 1, 1918

In the last week of September 1918 four separate major Allied offensives(25) were launched on the Western Front with the aim of finishing the war before the winter. In the second of these attacks the British First and Third Armies were to drive across the northern extension of the Hindenburg Line, towards

Figure 11 The Battle of the Canal du Nord

Cambrai.(26) The operation was a logical consequence Canadian success at Drocourt-Quéant and once again the Canadian Corps(27) was given a principal role in the renewed offensive. The task of crossing the formidable obstacle of the Canal du Nord(28) required the most careful planning(29) and precisely organised artillery and engineer support underpinned the success of the attack. At 5.20am, on Friday 27 September, following a night of heavy rain, assault troops of the Canadian 4th and 1st Divisions left their cramped assembly positions and attacked on a narrow front (centred on Sains-lez-Marquion) behind a devastating creeping barrage(30); Third Army's infantry, immediately to the right (south) advanced simultaneously. With dense clouds of smoke blowing towards the enemy lines the leading Canadian assault troops, assisted by tanks(31), quickly crossed the canal; Royal Engineers (32) immediately began bridging operations to speed troops, guns and supplies over the captured barrier for the next forward moves; the Marquion Line was passed later that morning and following much fierce fighting, the high ground of Bourlon Wood was in Canadian hands by nightfall; good progress was also made by Third Army. Attacks were renewed next day; though Canadian progress slowed, Third Army forces captured Noyelles, Marcoing, and Gouzeaucourt, and seriously threatened Cambrai.

In two days an advance of six miles was made on a twelve mile front; 10,000 enemy prisoners and 200 guns were taken. This spectacular success(33) represented a vital preliminary to Fourth Army's attack on the Hindenburg Line scheduled for 29 September.

(25) 'four separate major Allied offensives'

In the last week of September 1918 ambitious Allied plans to launch converging and co-ordinated blows against German forces on the Western Front were at last realised. Allied Commander-in-Chief, Marshal Foch, by now accepted Haig's view on the need for concerted convergent action: 'Foch began to think in terms of a series of violent and interrelated hammer blows with more lethal intentions than merely eliminating salients or freeing railwaysThe plans for separate attacks were drawn up by 23 September. The offensives themselves were to be launched on four successive days: 26 September—the American First Army and French Fourth Army would attack between the Meuse and Reims; 27 September—the British Third Army and the right of the British First Army were to attack in the Cambrai sector; 28 September—British Second Army, the Belgian Army and nine divisions of the French Army to attack in Flanders; 29 September—British Fourth Army and French First Army to assault the Hindenburg Position established behind the St Quentin canal. These offensives would give physical expression to Foch's inspirational battle cry 'tout le monde à la bataille' and coincide with welcome signs of impending general victory from other, more distant, theatres of war. 'In Salonika, the Bulgarians were about to request an armistice following a powerful Allied attack which had begun on 15 September. In Palestine the Turks were in retreat as a result of Allenby's breakthrough at Megiddo between 19 and 21 September.

> *four separate major Allied offensives-* ('Chronicles of the
> Great War. The Western Front 1914-1918', Peter Simkins,
> Godalming, Surrey, Bramley Books, 1997, p. 212).

(26) 'towards Cambrai'

With a curious and ironic symmetry by 27 September 1918 the British front lines now facing the Hindenburg Line, occupied familiar territory: ' . . . roughly, the line which the British Fifth and Third Armies had occupied before the German offensive of 21st March.' Reflecting the interdependency of the proposed British attacks, Haig specified that ' . . . the First Army [on the left] will attack on Z day [later fixed for 27 September] with a view to capturing the heights of Bourlon Wood in the first instance. It will then push forward and secure its left flank on the Sensée river and operate so as to protect the left of the Third Army . . . The Third Army will op in the direction of the general line Le Cateau-Solesmes. It will attack on Z Day in co-operation with the First Army and will press forward to secure the passage of the Canal de l'Escaut [Schelde Canal] so as to be in position to co-operate closely with Fourth Army on Z Day + 2 [29 September].'

> **'towards Cambrai'**—('Military Operations. France and
> Belgium, 1918' (Volume V), compiled by Brigadier-
> General Sir James E Edmonds and Lieutenant-Colonel R
> Maxwell-Hyslop, London, HMSO, 1947, p.1).

(27) 'Canadian Corps'

General Horne's instructions were issued on 18 September: 'The Canadian Corps was to force the passage of the Canal du Nord on a narrow frontage of about 2,500 yards where the canal was dry or had very little water in it, and then spread out to 9,700 yards and secure a line between the Schelde and the Sensée canals.'Whose force was, in addition to getting across the Canal du Nord, required ' . . . to take three strong and well wired trench systems, the Canal du Nord Line, about 300 yards east of the canal, the Marquion Line and the Marcoing Line'.

Currie, avoiding a direct assault on the more difficult section of the canal facing him, arranged his Corps to sidestep to the right (south, necessitating a southward extension of the corps boundary by over two thousand yards) so as to channel his attacking forces through a narrow frontage across a relative dry section of the canal.

> **Canadian Corps'**—('Military Operations. France and Belgium, 1918' Though the Canadian Corps was to be supported on its left by the British 11th (Northern) Division, these baldly stated requirements posed serious problems for Lieutenant-General Sir Arthur Currie (GOC Canadian Corps),

(28) 'Canal du Nord'

'The canal was under construction when the war broke out in 1914, large stretches of it were dry, the excavation had not everywhere been made to its full depth and the revetment had only been completed in certain parts . . . The British Armies in September,1918, were only concerned with the northern stretch— about thirty miles long—between the Somme and the Sensée. Its width and depth in this reach vary in different places. Its average width may be taken as 30 to 40 yards, and the average depth of the whole excavation in those parts where it had been completed as 30 to 40 feet, though in places where it passes through higher ground in cuttings it is as much as 60 feet deep . . . the Canal du Nord had water in it from the southern boundary of the Third Army at Manancourt past Etricourt and through the tunnel to a point south of Hermies. From here there was long dry stretch extending for nearly 7½ miles to 500 yards north of Inchy. From here to the northern end of the canal at its junction with the Sensée it again had water in it. Of the dry stretch of the canal, 10,500 yards was in the Third Army area, and 2,500 in the First Army area.

> **'Canal du Nord'**('Military Operations. France and Belgium, 1918' (Volume IV), compiled by Brigadier-General Sir James E Edmonds, London, HMSO, 1947, pp.424-426).

(29) 'careful planning'

Though never free from the attentions of German artillery, the period between the Drocourt-Quéant fighting and the assault on the Canal du Nord, allowed the Canadian Corps (as well as the other participating forces) to plan meticulously for the next phase of offensive operations. As well as setting reasonable objectives for the infantry, the problem of getting forces quickly and safely over the obstacle posed by the canal required the co-ordination of artillery, engineer and logistical support arms. Information obtained by the RAF of German defensive positions was of vital importance in the planning process. 'In preparation for bridging in the Canadian Corps and elsewhere, after air photographs had been studied, a depot of bridges of various lengths, ready and complete, was established, with a fleet of lorries standing by to take them forward as soon as reconnaissance reports were received and circumstances permitted.'

> **'careful planning'**—('Military Operations. France and Belgium, 1918' (Volume V), compiled by Brigadier-General Sir James E Edmonds and Lieutenant-Colonel R Maxwell-Hyslop, London, HMSO, 1947, p.21, f.n.1).

(30) 'creeping barrage'

'No preliminary bombardment was to be fired, but wire-cutting by the heavy artillery had begun on the 18th. The first phase was to be carried out under creeping barrages, with machine-gun barrages added, with three successive objectives; there was to be a halt of 50 to 105 minutes on the first and 34 to 50 minutes on the second . . . Bourlon Wood was to be enveloped by the 4th Canadian Division on the north and south, leaving the centre to be mopped up later.' Given that the infantry would be required to advance beyond the range of field guns, plans were put in place to provide continuing artillery support. In the fighting 27 September-1 October Canadian gunners used 'relay barrage fire': components of Divisional artillery brigades were rapidly pushed forward to offer continuing advanced cover for the infantry. Field guns were also hazarded in very close-support roles: gun teams, following on the heels of the attacking troops served the infantry, often over 'open sights'.

> **creeping barrage'**—('Military Operations. France and Belgium, 1918' (Volume V), compiled by Brigadier-General Sir James E Edmonds and Lieutenant-Colonel R Maxwell-Hyslop, London, HMSO, 1947, p.20

(31) 'tanks'

'The 7th Tank Battalion (Mark IV. tanks) was at the disposal of the Canadian Corps, and it allotted one company (8 tanks) to each of the 1st, 3rd and 4th Canadian Divisions. Tanks were not to be used beyond the third objective unless the advance was covered by a barrage.' Sixteen Mark IVs accompanied the initial assault and, in the circumstances, provided valuable support; having got across the canal (concealed from enemy anti-tank gun fire by billowing smoke on the battlefield) they ' . . . performed some useful work on the far side, helping to overcome wire and machine guns and making themselves especially useful in the clearance of Marquion. Five tanks, however, were knocked out by enemy fire and most of the others appear to have succumbed to mechanical difficulties by the end of the day.'

> **tanks'**—('Military Operations. France and Belgium, 1918' (Volume V), compiled by Brigadier-General Sir James E Edmonds and Lieutenant-Colonel R Maxwell-Hyslop, London, HMSO, 1947, p.20). ('Amiens to the Armistice. The BEF in the Hundred Days' Campaign, 8 August-11

November 1918', J P Harris (with Niall Barr), London, Brasseys, 1998, p.195).

(32) 'Royal Engineers'

Combining the roles of combat soldier and specialist technical support, Royal Engineer units (Canadian and British) provided crucial assistance for the assault. 'When the creeping barrage began to move forward, sappers followed directly behind the assaulting troops to repair roads and canal crossings, helping get guns forward', bridging small streams and waterlogged areas, clearing barbed wire, and fighting—destroying surviving enemy machine gun posts. (See: 'A Resource not to be Squandered: the Canadian Corps on the 1918 Battlefield', Bill Rawlings, in '1918: Defining Victory', edited by Peter Dennis and Jeffrey Grey, Canberra, Army History Unit, 1999. An eye-witness to the south, on Third Army's front, was full of praise for engineer support: ' . . . British batteries from the rear began to come by, to take fresh positions nearer the enemy. That they were able to cross the Canal du Nord so soon was due to the careful manner in which the battle had been thought out beforehand. A bridge had been built in sections, and the moment the German barrage had lifted that morning, the R.E.s were seen coming down from Hermes [sic] with the bridge lengths on wagons, and in a short time they had erected a trestle-way from bank to bank, over which guns and ammunition limbers were now pouring on to ground which scarcely an hour before was held by the enemy.

(33) 'spectacular success'

In extensive and complex fighting Third Army's formations—involving four Army Corps—successfully drove east and north-eastwards to threaten Cambrai. 'The Third Army on the 28th advanced a distance varying from 2,000 yards on the right to 5,000 yards on the left. It passed over the Marquion-Cantaing Line and part of the Hindenburg Support, and on the left reached the Schelde canal from Marcoing northwards to the Army boundary. The First Army made similar good progress, the right of the Canadian Corps, in line with Third Army, capturing the Marcoing

Line, whilst its left formed a flank reaching to the Sensée canal. Thus the two armies had in two days made a considerable breach, 12 miles wide and six miles deep into the German defences.

> **spectacular success'**—('Military Operations. France and Belgium, 1918' (Volume V), compiled by Brigadier-General Sir James E Edmonds and Lieutenant-Colonel R Maxwell-Hyslop, London, HMSO, 1947, p.46).

In what was perhaps the most complex, intricately-planned, and audacious assault of the war, the Canadian Corps used ladders to cross the Canal du Nord at a dry section of the ditch. Once across, they fanned out to outflank the German defences along the rest of the canal. The Germans abandoned the village of Bourlon and retreated to the Marcoing Line, just west of Cambrai. Over the next four days the Canadian Corps fought its way into the northwest corner of Cambrai, but here the attack stalled.

> From the Saskatchewan Dragoons website, *http://www. saskd.ca/skd-hon.htm*

The 46th Battalion was one of the lead battalions in the assault. They crossed the canal and took their initial objective, a sunken road six hundred yards beyond. The next day, the 46th continued the attack and took the Cambrai-Douai road, breaching the Marcoing Line at that point. The cost was 370 casualties. The 12th Brigade attacked through the battalion's lines on the 29th, and the 46th was withdrawn to the Divisional reserve for the remainder of the battle. The strength of the 46th Battalion on 30 September was 567 all ranks. They had taken more casualties in September 1918 than at Vimy Ridge and Passchendaele put together.

"On this day we buried all our hopes for victory."
War Diary of the German 188th Regiment, 27 September 1918

The 188th Regiment was tasked as the Bourlon garrison on the morning of 27 September.

Chapter 7

The Breaking of the Drocourt-Quéant Line, 2-3 September 1918

Figure 12 Drocourt-Quéant Line

Between 31 August and 1 September, while British artillery pounded the dense mass of wire entanglements shielding the Drocourt-Quéant Line(13), First Army's Canadian Corps paused to prepare and re-organise(14) prior to its next daunting forward move. With the aim(15) of breaking through the D-Q position, its three attacking infantry divisions (1st and 4th Canadian and 4th British) were provided with essential tank and air support(16).

Attacking at 5am on Monday 2 September(17), in early morning half-light, 1st Canadian Division(18) (going forward south-eastwards on the extreme right, south of the Arras-Cambrai road) and 4th Canadian Division(19) (in the centre, between Dury and the main road) led the assault up the exposed ridges, behind an

intense artillery barrage(20). On the left, the supporting British
4th Division(21) advanced south of the River Sensée. Tanks proved
invaluable in crushing paths through the dense barbed-wire and
dealing with strongpoints; despite heavy enemy machine-gun fire,
the first objectives (the front-system of the D-Q trenches) were
gained before 9am, and the follow-up battalions passed through
the leading attacking waves. Despite the obvious strength of their
field-defences enemy resistance varied considerably and large
numbers of German prisoners (22) were taken.

The second phase of the attack took the advance beyond the range
of artillery support and owed much to the infantry's courage and
tactical skill, as forward rushes, made by platoons and sections,
slowly gained ground within the D-Q support trenchlines. Despite
continuing heavy fighting (especially in the Buissy Switch), by
nightfall(23) it was clear that the Drocourt-Quéant Line had been
emphatically breached and Canadian Corps formations surged
into the open country beyond.

A general German retirement(24) took place during the night of
2/3 September and, on the following day, British forces cautiously
moved forward to within striking distance of their next objective—
the Canal du Nord.

(13) 'Drocourt-Quéant Line'

Known to the Germans as the 'Wotan Stellung', the Drocourt-
Quéant Line, by the British often shortened to the 'D-Q Position'),
'ran from a point in the Hindenburg Line about eleven miles west
of Cambrai, passing about seven miles west of Douai and joining the
main front east of Armentières.' Being effectively the northward
extension of the Hindenburg Line, it was arguably the strongest
system of field fortifications that the British Army has as yet come
up against. Though described as 'a line' it was in fact a position
of great depth incorporating several mutually supporting lines. It
comprised 'a front system and a support system, each with two
lines of trenches provided with concrete shelters and machine-
gun posts, and very heavily wired. The front line was ainly on the
crest, the support system on a reverse slope. Joining the Drocourt-

Quéant Line to the Hindenburg Support Line, and constructed in a similar fashion, was the important 'Buissy Switch' trench-line, which joined the Drocourt-Quéant Line along the forward slope of Mont Dury and the Arras-Cambrai road.

> **'Drocourt-Quéant Line'**—(History of the Corps of Royal Engineers' (Volume V), Chatham, The Institution of Royal Engineers, 1952, p.416, f.n.1).

(14) 'prepare and reorganise'

Recent heavy casualties and the immediate necessity of confronting a profoundly difficult obstacle understandably generated a concern in the Canadian Corps to get the next step right. Preferring caution to excessive haste a short pause was allowed for their preparations and the assault date put off until Monday 2 September. On Sunday 1 September, 1st Canadian Division units attacked Hendecourt Chateau and a notorious strongpoint called the 'Crow's Nest' (on a small hill to the north of the Chateau) in order to establish a better position for the main attack on the Drocourt-Quéant Line: both attacks (undertaken by 15th and 14th Battalions of 3rd Canadian Brigade) were successful, and held against enemy counter-attacks.

(15) 'the aim'

General Sir Arthur Currie's aim, stated simply, was to pierce the Drocourt-Quéant Line on a narrow front (astride the main Arras-Cambrai road) and then to spread his forces outwards to 'roll-up' the enemy to north and south. The battle's objectives were more formally summarised by the British Official Historian: 'The first objective was the line Cagnicourt-Dury-high ground south of Etaing, beyond the D.-Q. Support System. This having been gained, the advance was to be resumed at Zero+3 hours to the second objective, the high ground west of and overlooking the Canal du Nord and the Sensée marked roughly by Sains lez Marquion-Baralle-east of Ecourt St.Quentin-Recourt, and thence turning westwards, back to the first objective south of Etaing. First Army Commander, General Sir Henry Horne's original orders for the attack specified: that the 'Canadian Corps, with III Brigade Tank Corps, 1 regiment of cavalry and 17th Armoured Car Battalion attached will attack the D-Q Line on the 2nd September. The inclusion of cavalry in the forces available necessarily implied optimistic thoughts of breakthrough and exploitation.

> **'the aim'**—' ('Military Operations. France and Belgium, 1918' (Volume IV), compiled by Brigadier-General Sir James E Edmonds, London, HMSO, 1947, p.397).

(16) 'tank and air support'

By the standards of the earlier Battle of Amiens (8 August 1918) the tank support, available to the Canadian Corps for the Drocourt-Quéant Line attack was positively meagre, fifty vehicles—a number reflecting both the high demand for the use of armour by other formations on other fronts and the inevitable high losses and breakdowns incurred in the fighting to date. 'Two companies of Mark V tanks were allotted to each of the three attacking divisions and during the night of the 1st/2nd September the noise of their assembly was drowned by aeroplanes flying over the area.' Lavish in comparison, RAF support for the attack involved night-bombing of the defended villages, enemy billeting areas and airfields and 'On the day of the attack, No 8 Squadron co-operated with the tanks, No 73 dealt with anti-tank guns, No 6 co-operated with the cavalry, and Nos 5 and 52 with the attacking divisions.'

> **'tank and air support'**—('Military Operations. France and Belgium, 1918' (Volume IV), compiled by Brigadier-General Sir James E Edmonds, London, HMSO, 1947, p.397).

(17) 'Monday 2 September'

Complementing the Canadian Corps' advance, Third Army's XVII Corps moved forward later that morning, behind a tremendous artillery bombardment, to assault the southernmost sector of the Drocourt-Quéant Line. Indeed the morning of Monday 2 September, witnessed co-ordinated attacks along a broad front, from the River Sensée to the Somme: ' . . . All four corps of the Third Army and both the III Corps and the Australian Corps in Fourth Army were involved. The actions fought by Third and Fourth Armies were later designated part of the 'Battle of Bapaume'.

(18) '1st Canadian Division'

1st Canadian Division's attack was led (from right to left) by the 3rd and 2nd Canadian Brigades.

3rd Canadian Brigade: 16th and 13th Battalions advanced on a 1,600 yard front, well supported by the tanks and, despite problems with uncut wire, quickly overran the two trenches of the enemy front system.

Figure 13 Picture from Imperial War Museum

German resistance intensified and the follow-up units, 15th and 14th Battalions, pressed forward against considerable resistance, and the Bois de Bouche and village of Cagnicourt were taken. The Canadians were in the redoubtable Buissy-Switch position just after 11am but here faced the most difficult close and bloody fighting, which continued to well past nightfall.

2nd Canadian Brigade: 7th Battalion attacked on a 1,000 yard front against ferocious German machine-gun fire; the seven tanks assisting proved invaluable in suppressing some enemy posts; having gained the enemy's front system, 10th Battalion attempted to press on (around 8am) but was halted by intense small-arms fire. Between 4 and 5pm Villers-lez-Cagnicourt was captured, but the Canadians' progress within the Buissy-Switch was ferociously opposed south of the village 'and it was not until 11pm, after hand-to-hand fighting, that this trench was taken and a line consolidated beyond it.'

(19) '4th Canadian Division'

4th Canadian Division's attack was led by the 12th and 10th Brigades.

12th Canadian Brigade: 72nd, 38th and 85th Battalions advanced each on a 500 yard front and, assisted by tanks, quickly infiltrated the

Figure 14 '4th Canadian Division'

Drocourt-Quéant front and support systems; further progress, at the crest of the ridge, was held by enemy machine-gun and artillery fire.

10th Canadian Brigade: 47th and 50th Battalions with tank support, again made swift progress, gaining access to the enemy trench systems; 46th Battalion pushed through to take the village position of Dury.

Follow-up units of both Brigades passed through to continue the assault around 8am, but without artillery support and meeting firmer enemy resistance made little further progress.

(20) 'artillery barrage'

'Twenty brigades of field artillery and eleven of heavy artillery were to support the Canadian Corps' attack. The heavy artillery was to be used to engage bridges over the Canal du Nord and the River Sensée and for counter-battery work. The field artillery was to fire a deep, dense barrage moving forward at a rate of a 100-yard lift every three minutes, until it reached the forward edge of the main belt of barbed wire in front of the Drocourt-Quéant Line, at which point it was to slow to a rate of a 100-yard lift every five minutes. After 152 minutes the barrage would stop moving for half an hour, offering a protective barrier behind which the infantry would consolidate its gains.'

'artillery barrage'—('Amiens to the Armistice. The BEF
in the Hundred Days' Campaign, 8 August-11 November
1918', J P Harris (with Niall Barr), London, Brasseys,
1998, Amiens, pp.165-166).

(21) 'British 4th Division'

Two battalions of the 12th Brigade attacked on a 1,500 yard
frontage: 'Frontal resistance except from outposts which had
escaped the barrage, was, however insignificant, and the [2nd
Battalion] Essex and [1st] King's Own took both the D-Q systems
with comparatively light casualties and reached their first objective,
where the 2nd Lancashire Fusiliers reinforced them . . . Strong
opposition was met in the second phase of the operation, after
8am, when the 11th Brigade followed up but were held by enemy
fire and by evening ' . . . the 11th and 12th Brigades, somewhat
intermixed, held the D-Q Support System with the left flank bent
back through Prospect Farm south of Etaing.

'British 4th Division'—' ('Military Operations. France
and Belgium, 1918' (Volume IV), compiled by Brigadier-
General Sir James E Edmonds, London, HMSO, 1947,
p.402).

(22) 'German prisoners'

During the afternoon of 2 September Sir Douglas Haig visited
the headquarters of the Canadian Corps (at Noyelle-Vion) where
he was informed of the successful progress of the battle; he later
moved on to the HQ of the British 4th Division where he heard
reports on the state of morale of the enemy soldiers: 'The officer
examining the prisoners stated that the moral (sic) of the German
officers was terribly low. He had at no period of the war seen such
a despicable state. The prisoners I saw seemed well fed but badly
drilled.' On his subsequent visits to the HQs of 4th and 1st Canadian
Divisions Haig heard further reports on lowered enemy morale,
one of which stated 'that the German private soldiers abused their
officers and NCOs and would not obey their orders.'

'German retirement' ('Military Operations. France and Belgium, 1918' (Volume IV), compiled by Brigadier-General Sir James E Edmonds, London, HMSO, 1947, Note II, p.413).

(23) 'by nightfall'

Figure 15 Picture from Imperial War Museum

By the evening of 2 September, even though hand to hand fighting continued late into the night in some sections of the Buissy Switch trench (south of Villers-lez-Cagnicourt), it was clear that the German defences had been prised open: 'by dusk the Canadian Corps had ruptured the Drocourt-Quéant Line on a frontage of 7,000 yards, captured the Buissy Switch and the villages of Villers-lez-Cagnicourt and Cagnicourt and taken over 8,000 prisoners.' ('Amiens to the Armistice. The BEF in the Hundred Days' Campaign, 8 August-11 November 1918', J P Harris (with Niall Barr), London, Brasseys, 1998, p.167). But this splendid achievement was purchased at a high price in First Army casualties: in the first four days of September the Canadian Corps alone incurred an estimated 5,600 casualties (killed, wounded and missing).

(24) 'German retirement'

The breaking of the Drocourt-Quéant Position on the 2 September (together with the turning of the Somme resulting from the capture of Mont St Quentin and Péronne by the Australians further to the south) caused the German High Command the greatest consternation; plans for withdrawal were immediately issued (about noon on 2 September): ' . . . for the retirement behind the Sensée and the Canal du Nord and, farther south, to the Hindenburg Position, beginning that very night. The movement in the north was to pivot on the Scarpe near Etaing, but the new line was to run eastwards along the north bank of the Sensée to

near Arleux, whence it went southwards behind the Canal du Nord, west
of Bourlon Wood, to pick up the Hindenburg Line near Marcoing.

The Drocourt-Queant Line represented the west edge of the
Hindenburg Line. The Canadian 1st and 4th Divisions, assisted by
the British 52nd Division, took the line and advanced to the west
bank of the Canal du Nord.

> From the Saskatchewan Dragoons website, *http://www.
> saskd.ca/skd-hon.htm*

The 46th Battalion attacked through the Drocourt-Queant Line
on 2 September, took the village of Dury, and held it against
a German counterattack. The 46th suffered 320 casualties,
including Maj Rankin, who nevertheless remained on duty. In
turn they inflicted a large number of casualties on the Germans,
captured a 77mm field gun, 16 machine guns, and a small anti-
tank gun, and took over 400 prisoners. Included in the haul were
the German area commander, his assistant and medical staff,
and a large quantity of documents, which were captured when D
Company, attacking on the left, overran a German headquarters

The 46th was relieved on 4 September. They received over 150
replacements and conducted training until the 25th, when they
moved back into the line, relieving elements of the 25th and 26th
Battalions, and prepared to attack.

Chapter 8

The Battle of Valenciennes, 1-2 November 1918

By the end of October 1918 it was clear that Germany was losing the war(34). On the Western Front signs of disintegration(35) in her armies were increasing. Haig, convinced that another major blow might induce the German High Command to accept allied armistice terms before the end of the year, now planned a last great offensive(36). An essential preliminary for this operation was the capture of Valenciennes(37) to allow First Army's formations to progress to their designated jumping-off positions.

Figure 16 The Battle of Valenciennes

Well protected on the west by the Schelde Canal, the attack on Valenciennes took place, from the south. An initial assault by 51st Highland Division (38) on 28 October pushed the British line forward, despite determined German resistance, to Mount Houy(39), key feature to the defences of the city. The main phase of the assault, by the Canadian Corps(40) and British XXII Corps(41) (assisted on the right by Third Army's 61st

Division) began in the early morning of 1 November. Attacking at
5.15am, behind a huge artillery barrage(42), the 10th Canadian
Brigade(43) raced forward from Famars over Mount Houy and
northwards beyond; by 7am Aulnoy had fallen and the intact
bridge over the Rhonelle(44) secured. Progress was halted by
fierce machine-gun fire from Marly Steelworks. Meanwhile 12th
Canadian Brigade(45) had crossed the Schelde Canal and secured
footholds at the western corners of Valenciennes. By nightfall(46)
the Canadians had edged into Marly and were securely lodged
behind the line of the railway, just west of the city itself.

Attacks were renewed early next morning; Marly was occupied
and by 7.20am Canadian troops were in Valenciennes cautiously
following-up a rapid enemy withdrawal. The capture of the city
freed First Army(47) to move forward and align itself in readiness
to support Haig's planned great offensive on the Sambre, now
scheduled for 4 November.

(34) 'losing the war'

As the German armies were being battered and relentlessly
harried on the Western Front, German civilians were enduring
terrible sufferings at home, in the midst of food shortages and
economic, social and political upheavals. Germany's cause was
further weakened by defections and collapses among its war-weary
allies—Austria-Hungary, Bulgaria and Turkey: 'In Italy on the
24th [of October] the Battle of Vittorio Veneto had been begun
by successful spear-head thrusts of French and British troops;
in the Balkans hostilities with Bulgaria had ceased on the 30th
September, and the Allied forces were advancing through Serbia
and Albania; in the Palestine theatre, the pursuit was continuing
and Allied forces were nearing Aleppo; and in Mesopotamia the
British forces had just begun the advance on Mosul. By 29 October
the Austrian government had requested an armistice.

> losing the war'—('Military Operations. France and
> Belgium, 1918' (Volume V), compiled by Brigadier-
> General Sir James E Edmonds and Lieutenant-Colonel R
> Maxwell-Hyslop, London, HMSO, 1947, p.384).

(35) 'signs of disintegration'

The setbacks experienced by German forces on the Western Front by late October were, collectively, disastrous: 'By the 24th October the succession of heavy blows dealt by the British forces, coupled with the determined fighting of the American First Army in the Argonne at a very vital point of the enemy front in respect of his communications, had produced a cumulative effect, both moral

Figure 17 Picture from the Imperial War Museum

and material, upon the German Armies. Their difficulty in replacing the enormous losses in guns, machine guns and ammunition had increased with every fresh attack, and their reserves of men were practically exhausted . . . Although enemy troops could still be found to offer stout resistance from good cover, the infantry and machine-gunners were no longer reliable, and cases had been reported of their retirement without fighting ahead of the artillery barrage.' So saying the determined resistance offered by German forces at Valenciennes on 1 November moved Haig to comment in his diary that ' . . . the German Army is not yet demoralised!'

> **'signs of disintegration'**—('Military Operations. France and Belgium, 1918' (Volume V), compiled by Brigadier-General Sir James E Edmonds and Lieutenant-Colonel R Maxwell-Hyslop, London, HMSO, 1947, pp.383-4). ('Douglas Haig. War Diaries and Letters 1914-1918', edited by Gary Sheffield and John Bourne, London, Weidenfeld & Nicholson, 2005, p.484).

(36) 'last great offensive'

Haig was determined to give the German Armies no let up on the Western Front; he feared that a suspension of offensive operations would play into German hands—and allow them time to retire to a shortened defence line that might possibly be held until the spring of 1919. Foch certainly thought it was unlikely that victory could be secured before then. But the fighting on the Selle had dealt the German High Command a huge blow—Ludendorff resigned on 26 October partly as a result of this setback—and Haig sought to exploit the success by yet another, though far greater in scale, attack, that might 'bring about a collapse' of the enemy. Operational plans for this great battle (which required as a preliminary the taking of Valenciennes), were issued by British GHQ on 29 October: 'Z-Day' for the great attack on the Sambre was fixed for 4 November.Occupied by the Germans since 1914, the city of Valenciennes on the River Schelde (known in France as the River Escault) formed a crucially important communications centre and focal point for local German defences. By late October 1918 Valenciennes was crammed full of civilians (many of whom were refugees); acknowledging this fact (and in response to French government requests) British GHQ forbade direct bombardment of the city, the strong defences of which determined that the main British assault should be made principally (though not exclusively) from the south: 'The town was protected on the west side by the Schelde Canal, its width increased by floods, and the houses on the well-wired eastern bank bristling with machine guns so an infantry assault was out of the question. General Horne [GOC First Army] decided therefore to turn the town by the south, where the XXII Corps was already across the Schelde Canal.

> **'last great offensive'—'** ('Military Operations. France and Belgium, 1918' (Volume V), compiled by Brigadier-General Sir James E Edmonds and Lieutenant-Colonel R Maxwell-Hyslop, London, HMSO, 1947, p.455).

(37) '51st (Highland) Division'

At 5.15am on Monday 28 October the 4th Battalion the Seaforth Highlanders (51st (Highland) Division) attacked German positions on Mount Houy. Well supported by artillery and machine-gun barrage fire the Seaforths took the major enemy positions on the hill and pressed on to the railway west of Aulnoy (roughly a mile further north). But the operation, though successful, had resulted in heavy casualties and the weakened Scottish battalion was gradually forced to yield ground to repeated German counterattacks. The enemy regained the northern slopes and summit of the hill, leaving the Seaforths with only a precarious hold on the southern slopes by nightfall. German attacks continued the next day. The exhausted troops of the 51st Highland Division were relieved on the evening of 29 October by: (on the left), 4th Canadian Division's 10th Canadian Infantry Brigade and, (on the right), by 49th Division's 147th and 146th Brigades.

(38) 'Mount Houy'

Located directly north of Famars (and south-west of Aulnoy), Mount Houy, with its summit roughly 150 feet above the Schelde Canal, dominated the southern approaches to Valenciennes. The hill was a key position in the city's defences.

(39) Canadian Corps'

10th and 12th Canadian Infantry Brigades (4th Canadian Division), with 11th Canadian Brigade in support, were tasked with the main attack on Valenciennes on 1 November. 'It was subsequently settled . . . that the 10th Canadian Brigade (Br.-General J M Ross) should capture Marly and the southern outskirts of Valenciennes, and that as the attack advanced to a second objective some two thousand yards beyond the one already defined, the 12th Canadian Brigade (Br.-General J H MacBrien) from the west side of the Schelde canal should force its way into Valenciennes. The attack on Valenciennes was to be the Canadian Corps' last major offensive operation of the war.

> **Canadian Corps'—**' ('Military Operations. France and Belgium, 1918' (Volume V), compiled by Brigadier-General Sir James E Edmonds and Lieutenant-Colonel R Maxwell-Hyslop, London, HMSO, 1947, p.455).

(40) XXII Corps'

Immediately to the right, south, of the Canadian Corps, the British 49th and 4th Divisions of Lieutenant-General Sir A Godley's XXII Corps supported the Canadian attack. Infantry units of both 49th and 4th Divisions were west of the Schelde but to get forward in the assault needed to cross the Rhonelle 'stream'.

(41) 'huge artillery barrage'

The Valenciennes attack was notable for the devastating exploitation of superior artillery firepower in support of an infantry attack. Allied munitions production had provided British forces with near limitless quantities of artillery and ammunition (and British logistical support managed to get ordnance supplies to the front). The situation for German gunners could not have been more stark and contrasting.

The Canadian artillery plan for the attack was simple: 'to saturate every known German artillery position, every possible approach for German troops, and every likely assembly area for German reserves. The concentration of Canadian artillery fire meant that the protective 'creeping barrage', fired by 144 18-pounders and 48 4.5 howitzers, was of stupendous power: ' . . . the 18-pounders alone delivered seven tons of explosives per minute, on a front of less than a mile and a half . . . Ammunition expenditures were phenomenal . . . a grand total of 87,700 rounds, or 2,140 tons Commander of Canadian Artillery compared the bombardment with the 2,800 tons of shell both sides fired in the Boer War and the 37 tons expended at Waterloo, exclaiming that 'there had been nothing like it in the whole history of war for intensity.

> **huge artillery barrage'—'** ('A Resource not to be Squandered: the Canadian Corps on the 1918 Battlefield', Bill Rawlings in '1918: Defining Victory', edited by Peter Dennis and Jeffrey Grey, Canberra, Army History Unit, 1999, p.65).

(42) '10th Canadian Brigade'

'The 10th Canadian Bri-
gade sent forward the
44th and 47th Battalions
along the western side of
the Rhonelle . . . The early
part of the operation went
according to plan: Mount
Houy was carried and many
prisoners sent back; but
the enemy machine guns
held on to the Steelworks,
Marly and the southern
outskirts of Valenciennes,

Figure 18 '10th Canadian Brigade'

and the supporting artillery, especially that of the 5th Canadian
Division, suffered from the enemy's batteries . . . and from low-
flying air attacks. Towards noon the falling back of the left of the
49th Division exposed the right of the 10th Canadian Brigade, so
the 50th Battalion and six batteries of machine guns were used to
support it. It not only stood fast, but with the Canadian artillery
also assisted to repel the 4.30pm counter-attack against the 49th
Division. It was not until 10pm that patrols entered Marly . . . The
Steelworks, which the 49th Division should have taken, still held
out and continued to give trouble.

> **10th Canadian Brigade'—'** ('Military Operations. France
> and Belgium, 1918' (Volume V), compiled by Brigadier-
> General Sir James E Edmonds and Lieutenant-Colonel R
> Maxwell-Hyslop, London, HMSO, 1947, p.459).

(43) the Rhonelle'

The Rhonelle, variously described by the British Official Historian
as a 'stream' and a 'river', constituted an obstacle to the advance
of First Army's infantry on 1 November: 'The . . . stream is about
20 feet wide and 4 to 6 feet deep between Artres and Famars.
The enemy had a strong outpost line on the western side of the
Rhonelle (except near Artres, where the XVII Corps had a small

bridgehead); his main line was on the heights, about the line of the Préseau-Marly road."

> **the Rhonelle'**—('Military Operations. France and Belgium, 1918' (Volume V), compiled by Brigadier-General Sir James E Edmonds and Lieutenant-Colonel R Maxwell-Hyslop, London, HMSO, 1947, p.456).

(44) '12th Canadian Brigade'

The 38th and 72nd Battalions of the 12th Canadian Brigade attacked directly across the Schelde Canal and into Valenciennes. 'Three companies of the 38th Battalion had succeeded in crossing the Schelde canal in the early morning at the south-western corner of the town, and a platoon of the 72nd Battalion did so at the north-western corner. By noon the two battalions were across; but strong German opposition meant that the Brigade could not get farther than the railway on the western side of Valenciennes.'

> **12th Canadian Brigade'**—('Military Operations. France and Belgium, 1918' (Volume V), compiled by Brigadier-General Sir James E Edmonds and Lieutenant-Colonel R Maxwell-Hyslop, London, HMSO, 1947, pp.459-60).

(45) 'By nightfall'

By the end of the day's fighting on Friday 1 November Canadian forces had taken 1,400 prisoners, seven field guns ' . . . and over eight hundred enemy dead were counted. British 4th Division claimed 750 prisoners and on 49th Division's front 'Over three hundred German dead were counted, and a total of 15 officers and 790 other ranks, with about another hundred wounded, had been captured." Third Army's 61st Division took an additional 761 prisoners. British and Canadian casualties were, relatively speaking, low; the 10th Canadian Brigade reported 501 battle casualties for 1 November, of which only around 80 were reported as being killed.

'By nightfall'—' ('Military Operations. France and Belgium, 1918' (Volume V), compiled by Brigadier-General Sir James E Edmonds and Lieutenant-Colonel R Maxwell-Hyslop, London, HMSO, 1947, p.460).

(46) 'First Army'

Rapidly changing circumstances altered First Army's role in the planned great attack on the Sambre Canal: 'The XVII, XXII and Canadian Corps had reached their jumping-off line; but in consequence of the retirement of the enemy from the Schelde and the abandonment of Valenciennes, the set-piece planned by the First Army for the 4th November in conjunction with the Fourth and Third Armies was abandoned and orders given for the 11th and 56th Divisions (XXII Corps) to pursue, acting independently and with vigour' so as to deny the enemy opportunity for settling into an organised position.

This was Uncle Will's last battle, the battle took place at 5:15 in the morning the 46th or the Suicide Battalion was only at 40 % of its strength morning they were to go down the middle to Valenciennes with the canal on the west and a hill with machine guns on the other is. The 47th and 44th Battalions were to take the hill, and the 50th and 46th Battalions were to continue on to attack the city.

First Army'—' ('Military Operations. France and Belgium, 1918' (Volume V), compiled by Brigadier-General Sir James E Edmonds and Lieutenant-Colonel R Maxwell-Hyslop, London, HMSO, 1947, p.462).

"A" Company's Report on Valenciennes Operation—November 1st 1918

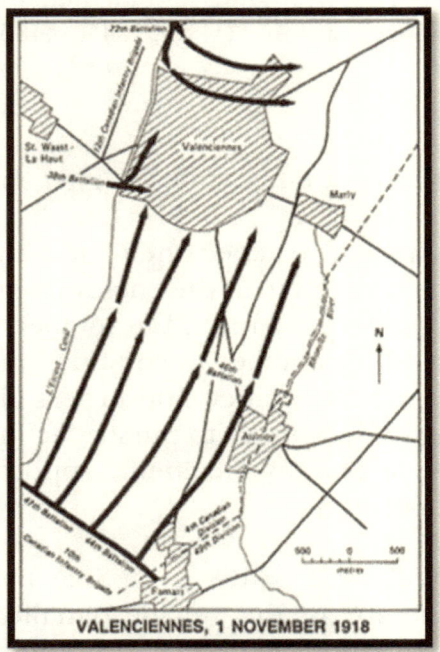

VALENCIENNES, 1 NOVEMBER 1918

The following is an extract from 46th Battalion War Diary for November 1918

" . . . *"A" Company attack on a two platoon frontage with one platoon in support. Lieut. Johnston with No. 1 Platoon on the right and Lieut. Cook with No. 2 Platoon on the left and Company Headquarters and Sergt Cairns with No. 3 Platoon forming the support wave and that we advance on lines of sections in file at forty paces interval and 100 paces distance, and that the Company advance behind the 44th Battalion with our right flank resting on the main FAMARS-VALENCIENNES road until the cemetery in AULNOY was reached, at which point the Company were to slightly change direction by swinging to the right and crossing the FAMARS-VALENCIENNES road and that they were to get in behind the 44th Battalion's left flank and taking care of all buildings on mainroad running out of AULNOY.*

The Battalion left present billets in THIANT for jumping off position by 0100 hours November 1st 1918 meeting guides and L.A.R.'s (**Lewis machine guns**) *at Railway cutting as set out in orders. From here guides* took respective platoons to their positions. Reported to B.H.Q. time 0255 hours that Company was in position. The barrage opened at 05:15 and the whole line moved off in good order. After we had gone about 500 yards we came under heavy machine gun fire from the left, just to the back of MOUNT HOUY and from the top of a building in K.3.c.40.30. I ordered one section of No.1 Platoon to mop up buildings which they did very satisfactorily, killing a large number of Boche and taking nine prisoners. The M.G. on the left still gave us considerable trouble but we got forward with very few casualties as the resistance was overcome during the advance to the sunken road by the leading waves of the 44th Battalion. When within 400 yards of the sunken road we encountered heavy machine gun fire from houses at junction on sunken road and main FAMARS-VALENCIENES road.

At this point the 44th Battalion had some trouble so I ordered No.1 Platoon to assist them overcoming their resistance. They captured some machine guns and many prisoners besides killing a great number. The advance then continued without any check until about 50 yards beyond the sunken road when direct machine gun fire was encountered from the trench and main road behind us. At this particular stage I only had about 20 men under my direct command as Lieut. Johnstone had taken something like 20 men with him who were now merged with "B" Company on the left. Realizing that I had not sufficient men to tackle the area allotted to "A" Company I called upon two sections of "C" Company, one to assist on the right flank and one on the left. The barrage playing here for 15 minutes enabled me to organize for the second stage and upon barrage lifting the line went forward in good order.

Opposition was not met with until we got practically in line with the houses at the junction of the roads in E.27.b.70.70. Here they held us up for a few minutes when the left L.A.R. section got their guns into action allowing the right to advance. The Boshe were now retiring down the sunken road to the brickfields and we bought to bear heavy fire from our L.A.R.'s and rifles on them which was very effective. The advance continued without further trouble until we reached the south side of the brickfields. At this point we came under very heavy machine gun fire and there was a fight on for over 20 minutes, when finally I ordered C.S.M. Gibbons, Sergt Cairns and 4 other ranks with 2 L.A.R.'s to outflank them on the right. These men crawled on their hands and knees while we covered them with rapid rifle and machine gun fire, resulting in them getting within 75 yards of the Boshe. The Boshe Officer *became a casualty and the whole position fell. We captured 3 field guns, one trench mortar, 7 machine guns and over fifty prisoners and the ground had plenty of dead on it. The advance then continued to the south edge of the factory without much opposition. Here I ordered Sergt Cairns with 8 other ranks and 1 L.A.R. to seize the railway crossing in E.16.c.85.30. I then went over to the right flank to straighten things out as this flank was held up by machine gun fire from the railway in E.23.a.60.20. I found nothing could be done by be as the fire came from the east of the river so I directed them to remain where they were until the situation cleared on the left. I proceeded to the left and met Lieut. Johnstone coming over with 10 O.R's (ordinary ranks) and two L.A.R.'s of "A" Company and 20 other ranks of the 44th Battalion he had taken charge of. He was proceeding to rejoin the Company. I ordered Lieut. Johnstone to mop up the factory and established posts on the railroad, while I proceeded to the left to find out how Sergt Cairns had made out. Sergt Cairns had established a post covering all the approaches and was then moving down the railway to connect with Lieut. Johnstone. The situation here was now clear. I once more went to the right to see if the bridgehead could not be taken but found a very limited field of fire and not a satisfactory position to be taken up so retained the position in E.22.b.60.00. The whole line was established by 0900 hours.*

I then notified Lieut. Jones of "C" Company to have patrol report to me at once (as per O.O.181 of Oct.31/18). Lieut. MacLeod reported to me and I gave him the necessary instructions and he moved his party forward at 0920 hours. With him were 1 Sergt, 10 O.R's with L.A.R. They entered the factory just the other side of the railway in E.16.c.90.40. Lieut. MacLeod left 7 O.R's in the houses while he and Sergt Cairns and 2 O.R's with L.A.R. proceeded to examine factory, Sergt Cairns handling the gun himself. Just as they were crossing the street a Boshe opened on them with an automatic rifle. Sergt Cairns made a run for the swinging door opening into the courtyard shooting his L.A.R. from the hip. Those he did not kill or wound ran down a back street. At this time Lieut. MacLeod and one O.R. entered the courtyard and as they proceeded around the corner they discovered about 50 more Boshe in a passage in a south-easterly end of the yard. Here they ordered them to put up their hands which was done immediately with the exception of one Boshe who retained his rifle. Lieut. MacLeod immediately covered him with his revolver when a Boshe Officer made a motion as if to put the rifle aside at the same time drew his pistol and shot Sergt Cairns through the stomach. Sergt Cairns then opened fire from the hip killing and wounding about 30. The

Boshe then saw they must fight for their lives and commenced firing a machine gun from a high brick wall. Sergt Cairns was again hit through the wrist but continued to fire his L.A.R. when he finally got a bullet through his hand nearly taking it off. This bullet also broke the L.A.R. He then threw the L.A.R. in the face of one of the Boshe who were firing at him, knocking him over. He then staggered to the gateway and collapsed. He was being carried back to our line when M.G. fire opened from the left killing one of the carrying party. Lieut. MacLeod then dragged him into our lines and reported to me at 1315 hours what he had done and reported casualties as 1 killed and 1 wounded.

At 1800 hours same date two platoons of 50th Battalion came up to reinforce. These consisted of 2 Sergts and 23 O.R.'s.

At 2100 hours I was relieved by a Company of the 54th Battalion and I reported with Company to THIANT.

In conclusion would say the barrage was splendid though there were a number of shorts during the latter stages of the advance. The smoke barrage was effective and enabled us to get close to the Boshe, and preventing him from knowing our strength which, had he known, would have caused us considerably more trouble and more casualties. The men did all I expected of them and I wish to specially mention the valuable services throughout the entire operation of the following O.R.'s.

> *Sergt Cairns*
> *C.S.M. Gibbons*
> *Privates Slack, Dennis, and Windrim*
> *Also Lieut. MacLeod of "C" Company*

I consider the work done by the above mentioned greatly assisted in the success in the action of my Company.

> *Total casualties;—All ranks—42*

R.W. Gyles Capt.
C.C. "A" Company

. . ."

Another account of the Valenciennes Operation can be found in the story of Sergeant Cairns where he won the last Victoria Cross of WW1. what it was like that days is the story of Sergeant Cairns, taken from the internet website of the Saskatchewan Dragoons, *http://www.saskd.ca/skd-hon.htm*

It was dark, with occasional splashes of rain, on Halloween night, 1918, when the Canadians moved down from billets in Thiant to the front line for the attack on the French city of Valenciennes. After repeated failures on the part of the imperial troops, the taking of the city was entrusted to the men from Canada, and the task was given to the 4th Division.

The Canadians had advanced down the west side of the Canal l'Escaut early in October, until they had reached a position opposite Valenciennes. The enemy dammed the river lower down and flooded the area around the city. For three weeks the two armies viewed each other across the watery expanse with no other excitement than occasionally sniping at each other. Then the orders came to the Canadians to move back for an attack on the city from the south.

The Dominion troops appreciated the honour implied in the changed orders giving them the task of taking Valenciennes, and to keep the spirits of the men to a higher pitch, word was received the day before the attack that Austria had signed the armistice. Thoughts of the end of the war and home made them eager to make a quick finish of the work at hand.

The men moved to the assembly trenches and took up battle formation under cover of darkness. The 10th Brigade frontage extended from Trith St. Leger, on Canal l'Escault to Famars, the canal forming the left boundary of the area to be attacked, and the Rhonelle river, the right boundary. The 46th Battalion, holding the right sector of the brigade frontage, from La Fontenelle farm to Famars joined with imperial troops across the Rhonelle.

The attack opened with a heavy artillery and smoke barrage before dawn. The first wave of infantry went over the top and advanced to its objective, capturing Mount Houy, a steep wooded hill, strongly held, which has proved fatal to several previous attacks. When the leading battalion had reached Aulnoy the 46th Battalion passed through and carried the attack to the final objective, the main railway in Valenciennes. There was hard fighting in Aulnoy and down the two rural streets connecting Aulnoy and Famars with Valenciennes. The streets were closely packed on either side with houses, from which the Boche attacked the passing troops. Small mopping up squads were formed in the Canadian line and these houses cleaned out, the men fighting from house to house down the long street. The number of prisoners taken in this operation was greatly in excess of the attacking force, the 46th Battalion alone taking 800 prisoners with a force of not more than 300 men.

Sgt. Cairns was in charge of a platoon during the advance. About 300 yards north of Aulnoy, when he was advancing down the Famars road, a machine gun opened on his men from a house on the side of the street. The fire was coming from a window upstairs. Sgt. Cairns seized a Lewis gun and rushed into the house. Dashing upstairs in face of fire turned on him, he killed the crew of five and captured the gun. The Canadian line advanced. It swung across the Famars road to the south side where, in front of an old French cemetery, they were held up again by fire from a strongly-held machine gun post.

Again Sgt. Cairns rushed forward alone, firing his gun from the hip as he went. He silenced and captured and sending back scores of prisoners.

The Germans, seeing the Canadian officer and the sergeant with his Lewis gun, threw up their hands when ordered but before they could be disarmed one of them gave the signal that the two men were alone and, as he approached Sgt. Cairns as if to surrender, a German officer drew his pistol and shot Cairns through the stomach. Sgt. Cairns immediately dropped to his knees and fired upon the German officer, killing him instantly. The other Boche then took cover behind boxes and piles of debris and began firing on the two Canadians. In spite of the fact that he had received his fatal wound, Cairns got his gun into action. Again he was wounded in the hand and arm, but bleeding and in great pain he continued to operate his gun. Then another shot blew away the trigger and mangled his hand. Twenty Boche ran forward to overpower him. Seizing his broken gun, he hurled it into the face of the nearest Hun, then staggering to the gate, collapsed unconscious.

In a moment the remainder of the patrol came running to the courtyard and a skirmish took place, during which Lieut. MacLeod dragged away the insensible form of the hero, placing him on a door to use as a stretcher. During this evacuation enemy fire was taken from the flank killing one of the stretcher bearers and wounding Sgt. Cairns yet again. They carried him back to the Canadian line and then to the field hospital where he died the next day.

Now taken from J,M, Ross Brigadier—General 10th Canadian Infantry Brigade, Narrative of Operations Second Battle of Valanciennes November 1, 1918. Dated November 13, 1918.

At the end of this report General Ross *wrote "with the splendid success of the 10th Canadian Infantry Brigade operations on November 1st was concluded probably the finest and most satisfying engagement in which this Brigade has ever been employed"*

On 1 Nov, the 46th Battalion—at this point only 405 strong—mingled with the 44th Battalion during the initial advance, then continued into the city alone. Together with the 44th, they killed over 800 Germans and took 800 prisoners from five infantry and two machine gun regiments. In addition, the 46th captured seven field guns, six mortars, two anti-tank guns, and 45 machine guns. The 46th suffered 126 casualties—over 30% of the men who started the attack. Included in this number was Sergeant Hugh Cairns, who won, posthumously, the last Canadian Victoria Cross of the war.

Chapter 9

November 1-11 The End

The Germans fought a series of small rear-guard actions between Valenciennes and Mons, Belgium, which Canadian troops entered before the Armistice was signed on 11 November 1918, ending the war.

These were the battles that both took part in, I am sure that if I outlined like this all of the battles that each of them took part in it would tell the same story, of hardship, mud, and death. Which brings me to my next question I asked myself is why? Why did two farmers for Ontario, join and go aboard and live and die in these conditions. William was 29 and Robert was 27, both old enough to know, war was hell.

Rates of Pay

Privates in the CEF during the Great War received $1.10 a day for the time that they were serving. This was significantly lower than the normal pay that a man employed in manual labour would receive, and well below the amount required to provide for a wife and children. To compensate for this, the Canadian Government provided a "Separation Allowance" for men who could prove that they had dependants, normally restricted to a wife or mother where they were the sole wage earner. This separation allowance varied from $20 per month for Privates to $60 per month for senior officers. Even with the separation allowance, the amount of money provided to a soldiers dependants was insufficient, which led to the creation of a "Patriotic Fund", a charity that provided additional money to help tide a family over while their husband or son was overseas. The Patriotic Fund had no fixed schedule. The amounts provided were determined on a case by case basis.

Rank	Basic Pay (per day)	Overseas allowance (per day)	Separation Allowance per month
Major General	$ 20.00	$ 4.00	$ 60.00
General Staff Officer—1st Grade	$ 10.00	$ 3.00	$ 60.00
General Staff Officer—2nd Grade	$ 8.00	$ 3.00	$ 60.00
Assistant Director of Medical services	$ 8.00	$ 3.00	$ 60.00
Chief Paymaster	$ 8.00	$ 3.00	$ 60.00
General Staff Officer—3rd Grade	$ 5.00	$ 3.00	$ 60.00
Divisional Paymaster	$ 5.00	$ 3.00	$ 60.00
ADC to Commander	$ 3.00	$ 3.00	$ 40.00
Brigade Commander	$ 9.00	$ 3.00	$ 60.00
Brigade major	$ 6.00	$ 3.00	$ 60.00
Colonel	$ 6.00	$ 1.50	$ 60.00
Lieutenant-Colonel	$ 5.00	$ 1.25	$ 60.00
Major	$ 4.00	$ 1.00	$ 50.00
Captain	$ 3.00	$ 0.75	$ 40.00
Lieutenant	$ 2.00	$ 0.60	$ 30.00
Paymaster	$ 3.00	$ 0.75	$ 40.00
Quartermaster	$ 3.00	$ 0.75	$ 40.00
Warrant Officer	$ 2.00	$ 0.30	$ 30.00
Quartermaster-Sergeant	$ 1.80	$ 0.20	$ 25.00
Orderly Room Clerk	$ 1.50	$ 0.20	$ 25.00
Squadron, Battery, Company Sergeant-Major	$ 1.60	$ 0.20	$ 25.00
Squadron, Battery, Company Quartermaster Sergeant	$ 1.50	$ 0.20	$ 25.00
Colour Sergeant, staff Sergeant	$ 1.60	$ 0.20	$ 25.00
Sergeant	$ 1.35	$ 0.15	$ 25.00
Corporal	$ 1.10	$ 0.10	$ 20.00
Bombardier or 2nd Corporal	$ 1.05	$ 0.10	$ 20.00
Trumpeter, Bugler, Drummer	*$ 1.00*	*$ 0.10*	*$ 20.00*
Private, Gunner, Driver, Sapper, Batman, Cook	$ 1.00	$ 0.10	$ 20.00

Reasons for Stoppages of pay

1. Absent without leave
2. In hospital for drunkenness
3. In hospital for self-inflicted wound
4. In custody for any offence against the Army Act
5. In custody for drunkenness
6. In hospital with venereal disease

As you can see by the chart my two uncles made $ 401.50 a year. As a "helper" on a farm in 1916 they would have made $396.88 for the same period of time. Their income could have been the same staying home! So if it was not money that called the men to the front what was it? Patriotism? Duty?

World War One—Statistics

The First World War, also known as the "Great War" or the "War to End All Wars," was global war.

- Battles were fought in the trenches using machine guns, poisonous gas and tanks
- Battles were fought at sea and coastal towns were shelled by German warships
- Planes were used for battle and for positioning and reporting on the enemy
- Battles were fought by air with many air raids by German Zeppelins
- Civilian workers produced weapons, munitions, equipment and supplies for the troops
- Medical personal ministered to the hundreds of thousands of wounded, maimed and sick

Allied Countries—Losses:

Military Casualties:	5.7 million
Civilian Casualties:	3.67 million
Military Wounded:	12.8 million

Allied Countries Involved in WWI

Great Britain	Canada	United States	France	Greece	India
Australia	New Zealand	Russia	Italy	Serbia	South Africa

Central Powers - Losses:

Military Casualties:	4.02 million
Civilian Casualties:	5.2 million
Military Wounded:	8.42 million

Central Powers Countries Involved in WWI

Germany

Austria-Hungary

Bulgaria

Ottoman (Turkey) Empire

Global WWI Losses:

Military Casualties: 9,720,450

Civilian Casualties: 8,865,650

Military Wounded: 19,769,102

Military Firsts of WWI:

Trench Warfare

Airships & Planes

Tanks, Trucks & Submarines

Wireless Communication (Telegraph)

Machine Guns & Long Range Artillery

Chemical Warfare (poisonous gas) & Flame Throwers

Estimated Cost of WWI

(for each of the major countries involved)

Country	Troops Deployed	Killed	Wounded	War Cost in Dollars
Germany	11,000,000	1,773,700	4,216,058	$37,775,000,000
Russia	12,000,000	1,700,000	4,950,000	$22,293,950,000
Great Britain	8,905,000	908.371	2,090,212	$35,334,012,000
United States	4,355,000	126,000	264,000	$22,625,253,000
France	8,410,000	1,357,800	4,266,000	$24,262,583,000
Belgium	267,000	13,716	44,686	$1,154,468,000
Canada	619,500	66,655	172,950	$1,665,576,

Picture of the original headstone taken November 3, 1918.

"The Present Headstone"

Name—FYFE WILLIAM CLIFFORD

Rank: Private

Regiment/Service: Canadian Infantry (Saskatchewan Regiment)

Unit Text: 46th Bn.

Date of Death:01/01/1918

Service No:782337

Eldest Son of John and Annie Fyfe of Richards Landing Ontario

Cemetery: Aulnoy Communal Cemetery

I believe Uncle Will was killed from Machine Gun fire early afternoon November 1, 1918, Some of the family said that Annie Fyfe his mother received a letter saying he died in hospital from infection from his wounds. If this was true it was from wounds he received that afternoon, both his headstone and death certificate say he died November 1, 1918. With the original picture of the headstone was taken on November 3, 1918.

My brother Rick told me once: *"a person is never dead as long as there is one person who can still remember them"*. This was the very purpose of this book, to make William and Robert Fyfe live on. The Aulnoy Cemetery is 3.5 kilometres from the Town of Valenciennes, that would put him back to just about where he was shoot.

When I started this project I wanted to know why would these people join, go overseas and fight a war, in a country that he/she does not even know. However, as I progressed the answer was not as important anymore. What had become important was that both my Uncles be remembered Robert who was wounded and William who was killed, be recognized by their family for what they did for their country.

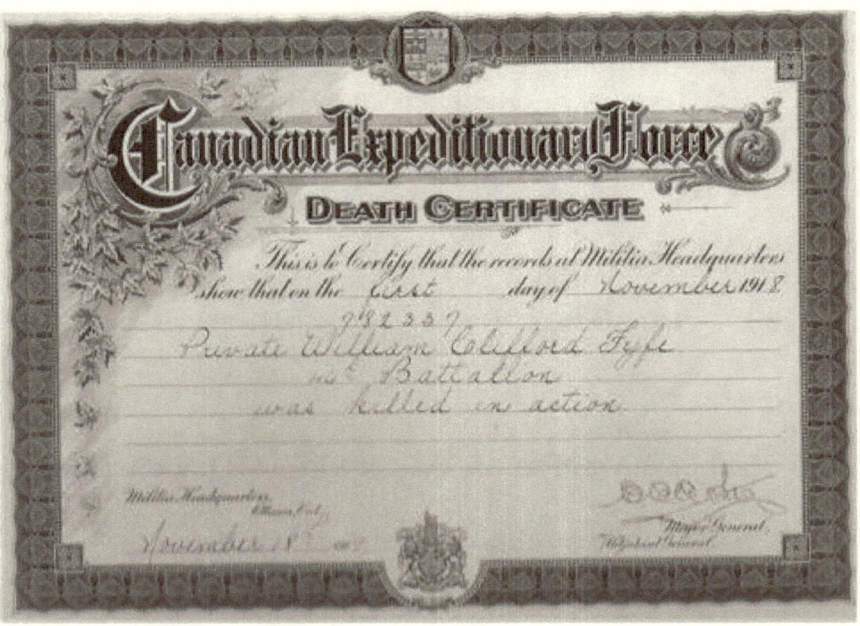

Bibliography

Berton, Pierre, *Marching As To War*, Canada: Anchor Canada, 2001

Giesler, Patricia, *Valour Remembered*, Ottawa: Department of Veterans Affairs, 1982

Gilbert, Martin, *The First World War*, New York: Henry Holt and Company, 1994

Marteinson, John et al, *We Stand On Guard*, Montreal: Ovale Publications, 1992

McWilliams, James L. and Steel, R. James, *The Suicide Battalion*, Edmonton: Hurtig Publishers, 1978

Morton, Desmond, and Granatstein, J.L., *Marching to Armageddon*, Toronto: Lester & Orpen Dennys Limited, 1989

Natkiel, Richard, *Atlas of Battles*, New York: The Military Press, 1984

Nicholson, Colonel G.W.L., *Canadian Expeditionary Force 1914-1919*, Ottawa: Queen's Printer, 1964; published on the Internet by the Directorate of History and Heritage

Young, Brigadier Peter, with Calvert, Brigadier Michael, *A Dictionary of Battles 1816-1976*, New York: Mayflower Books, 1977

War Diaries—46th Canadian Infantry Battalion; published on the Internet by The National Archives of Canada: *10 August 1916-30 September 1917*; *1 October 1917-30 September 1918*; and *1 October 1918-30 April 1919*

www.flandersfieldsmusic.com/thepoem.html

Veterans Affairs Canada
www.vac-acc.gc.ca/rememberseterans Affairs